The Beauty and Glory of Christian Living

The Beauty and Glory
of Christian Living

Edited by
Joel R. Beeke

Reformation Heritage Books
Grand Rapids, Michigan

Published by
Reformation Heritage Books
2965 Leonard St. NE
Grand Rapids, MI 49525
616-977-0889 / Fax 616-285-3246
e-mail: orders@heritagebooks.org
website: www.heritagebooks.org

Printed in the United States of America
14 15 16 17 18 19/10 9 8 7 6 5 4 3 2 1

Library of Congress Cataloging-in-Publication Data

The beauty and glory of Christian living / edited by Joel R. Beeke.
    pages cm
  Includes bibliographical references.
    ISBN 978-1-60178-335-6 (hardcover : alk. paper) 1. Christian life. I. Beeke, Joel R., 1952-
    BV4501.3.B424 2014
    248.4—dc23
                           2014018226

For additional Reformed literature, request a free book list from Reformation Heritage Books at the above address.

With heartfelt appreciation for

Ann Dykema

my faithful and loyal administrative assistant
who works hard, promptly, and efficiently,
often going beyond the call of duty.

Contents

Preface

On November 21, 1637, the Puritan divine Samuel Rutherford wrote to a dear friend, "The world knoweth not our life; it is a mystery to them."[1] To those who, like Rutherford, know firsthand how sweet it is "to be wholly Christ's, and wholly in Christ,"[2] the Christian life can be described as nothing short of being both beautiful and glorious.

This book consists of the addresses given at the 2013 Puritan Reformed Conference on the beauty and glory of Christian living. The addresses are organized under three headings: 1) Christian Living in Its Divine Roots, 2) Christian Living in Its Human Branches, and 3) Christian Living in Its Earthly Storms.

The first section considers the divine source of the Christian life. In chapter 1, Michael Barrett leads us through an exposition of Colossians 3:1–17. Here we are reminded that for the Christian, "the more we know the gospel and our completeness in Christ, the more we can enjoy and experience the gospel in life." Ian Hamilton develops this theme further in chapters 2 and 4. He answers the question, What precisely is the Spirit's sanctifying, beautifying ministry? and concludes that the "Spirit does not mortify sin without our cooperation. He blesses or prospers our striving, but He does not bless our sloth." In chapter 4, Hamilton further develops this idea by addressing the means by which God beautifies His children. He points out that Jesus Christ is God's beautifying template whereby His children are conformed to Him. In chapter 3, John Tweeddale enlarges upon the theme

---

1. Samuel Rutherford, *Letters of Samuel Rutherford*, ed. Andrew A. Bonar (London: Oliphant Anderson & Ferrier, 1891), 530.
2. Rutherford, *Letters*, 13.

of spiritual-mindedness by focusing on John Owen's "two basic motivations: 'zeal for God's glory and compassion for men's souls.'"

The second section considers God's work in believers in three practical areas: the family, the workplace, and in evangelism. In chapter 5, Joel Beeke considers the Puritan William Gouge's practical views on marriage and child-rearing, showing that in some ways the Puritans are far ahead of us in their biblical understanding of family. In chapter 6, William VanDoodewaard addresses the issue of the Christian in the workplace, drawing our attention to 1 Peter 2:18–25. VanDoodewaard concludes that for the Christian, "Jesus' perfect example and His humble suffering" is the supreme motivation for believers to work for His glory. Rounding out the second section in chapter 7, Brian Najapfour presents five reasons that followers of Christ are to be evangelistic and five common excuses for not being evangelistic.

The final section challenges us to consider the beauty and glory of Christian living in the midst of life's trials and afflictions. In chapter 8, Gerald Bilkes gives us ten reasons "why we ought not to think God's fiery furnace strange." In chapter 9, Brian Croft provides husbands with three lessons to consider when exploring the biblical model for marriage: flee the adulterous woman, delight in your wife, and tremble before God. Then, in chapter 10, David Murray draws our attention to the joyful words of the apostle Paul in Philippians 4:8. Believers in all ages worry, Murray admits, "but Paul holds out the prospect of an unimaginable and unsurpassable divine peace to garrison our hearts and minds, a peace that patrols the entrances to our emotions and thoughts." Christians, therefore, are called to change what feeds their minds.

In chapter 11, Brian Croft draws on Mark 5 to find hope in times of sickness, suffering, and death, counseling us to "hold fast to our sovereign Savior, knowing He is our hope, our joy, and the One who rules over all circumstances of our sickness and even our death for the good of His people, for the display of the gospel, and the glory of His great name." In the final chapter, John Tweeddale provides us with a sweeping view of the book of Judges, focusing both on the devastating consequences of sin and the tenacity of divine grace.

This book, like the conference, affirms that the Christian life begins and ends in the free and sovereign grace of God in Christ.

We are grateful for all of the individuals who helped to organize the conference and the publication of this book. We are also thankful for each of the speakers who participated in the 2013 Puritan Reformed Conference and who gave us permission to publish their addresses. Most of all, we are humbly grateful to the triune God, "who hath blessed us with all spiritual blessings in heavenly places in Christ" (Eph. 1:3).

—Joel R. Beeke and Chris Hanna

CHRISTIAN LIVING IN ITS DIVINE ROOTS

CHAPTER 1

Living Out Our Faith:
The Christian Life Inside Out

Michael Barrett

Colossians 3:1–17

Many Christians have a problem with the Christian life. Faith loses its attractiveness. Initial enthusiasm dwindles and disillusionment sets in. For some, Christianity is just a set of beliefs; for others, it is a rigid set of standards. Nearly every new movement or seminar for success is an effort to capitalize on the dissatisfaction of Christians who have somehow failed to understand what the Bible says about the Christian life. There is a practical side to doctrine, and Scripture inseparably links believing and living.

It amazes me that the truths that so overwhelmed the thinking of first-century Christians never seem to cross the minds of twenty-first-century believers. There is in the gospel a dynamic to energize and guide life along the proper paths. It is only when Christians ignore the gospel that they find Christianity a drudgery. Too often, belief in the gospel is reduced to a past decision rather than elevated and centralized into a corpus of truth that is the constant object of present faith and application. All of life, for the Christian, ought to be squarely focused on Christ. Christ, His cross, and the completeness of His gospel must interfere with life; the gospel must be the focal point for living out our faith. It must stand in the way of every sin and point the way to piety. It is always the case that right thinking about the gospel produces right living in the gospel.

Colossians 3:1–17 makes this connection. In the previous chapter, Paul exposes and warns against all the additions to Christ that are supposed to lead to spiritual attainment and satisfaction. He does so by expounding the completeness of Christ in terms of His deity and humanity (2:9) and the believer's completeness in Him in terms of union (v. 10). Significantly, the words *fullness* and *complete* are from the same Greek root. Paul's play on words underscores the wonder of the truth itself. Our completeness is in union with Christ, not in how we adhere to religious rituals or other manifestations of "will worship" (v. 23).

In Colossians 3, Paul builds on the theology of throne-union with Christ and looks at the Christian's life from two perspectives—inside and outside. The apostle defines the principle for Christian living and then the procedure for living it. Our text is a classic example of how deep theology translates into the practice of life. I think it was Charles H. Spurgeon who said this chapter begins in heaven and ends in the kitchen. Paul's logic is clear in proving once again that we are complete in Christ.

Therefore, I want to consider the text from these two perspectives: the principle for Christian living and the procedure for Christian living—the hidden life and the seen life.

The Principle: The Hidden Life

In the opening four verses, Paul expounds the theology that is essential and foundational to both spiritual life and godly living. He draws our attention to the objective realities of the believer's union with Christ, with all of its representative, vital, intimate, and mystical significance. This union is equally true for every genuine believer in Jesus Christ, but is not equally enjoyed or consciously experienced by all. Hence, he directs us how to think in the light of the facts. Three thoughts stand out about the believer's hidden life.

The Fact of the Hidden Life

Verse 3 declares the proposition: "For ye are dead, and your life is hid with Christ in God." This is indisputable fact. The text more literally reads, "You died." Since he is writing to those who were very much alive physically, this past death refers to something spiritual, something, dare I say, mystical. Don't be afraid of this word, so long as you confine it within biblical limits. Theologically, it refers to spiritual truth that surpasses human comprehension because of the transcendence of its nature and significance. It is a most appropriate word to designate our union with Jesus Christ, a truth that, notwithstanding its reality, defies explanation. The statement "You died," then, takes us to that mysterious and mystical union of every believer with Jesus Christ in His death on the cross.

There is a sense, though incomprehensible, in which every believer jointly participates and shares in the work of the Lord Jesus. This staggers the mind. Consider these astounding statements that declare the believer's communion with the death of Christ: "I am crucified with Christ" (Gal. 2:20); "We are buried with him by baptism into death" (Rom. 6:4; Col. 2:12); "Our old man is crucified with him" (Rom. 6:6); and "If one died for all, then were all dead" (2 Cor. 5:14; i.e., all for whom He died, died). Obviously, we did not hang on the cross along with Christ to suffer all the agony and torment that He endured in both body and soul. In the physical sense, Christ suffered and died alone as the substitute for His people. He bore the penalty of our sin and exempted us from ever having to pay it. He is our Federal or Representative Head, who stands in our place, and we were, thus, united to Him. When Christ died, all of His people died with Him. God regarded believers—His elect and Christ's inheritance—as being in His Son.

It was on the cross where satisfaction for our sin was secured and where our connection to sin was severed. Being crucified with Christ means that we should look down on sin and the old life from that vantage. Sin that is so alluring when it is in our face loses its appeal when we view it from the old rugged cross.

Ironically, although we died, our life has been hidden with Christ in God. This mystical death did not produce a lifeless corpse. On the contrary, our union with His death always includes union with His resurrection and life. Consider verse 1, which assumes that believers were raised with Christ. Community with Him in His death always includes community with Him in His life.

Significantly, Paul uses a different form of verb to express the hidden life. Whereas Paul says we died once for all, the form of the verb *hid* addresses both the past act of being hidden and its continuing consequences. When we died with Christ, we were at that very time hidden in Christ, and there we constantly remain. Given that Christ is sitting at the right hand of God (v. 1), this is all the more remarkable. He's in heaven; we're in heaven in Him. By faith, we are to know and reckon for ourselves that we are in Him.

The implications and applications of this throne-union are far-reaching, both regarding our security with God and our duty in the world. The world can't see us there (after all, we're hidden), but God does because all things are open before His eyes. The Head-body analogy is one way Paul describes union with Christ (1:18). It is our security that God sees the body through the Head; it is our duty that the world sees the Head through the body. It is sobering to realize that the world's estimation of the Head is so often determined by what it perceives about the body. That makes a huge difference in how we live out our faith.

The Imperatives of the Hidden Life
Paul issues two imperatives in verses 1 and 2 that are the logical corollaries to his proposition regarding the believer's union with Christ. The logic is clear from the opening statement, which assumes the reality of fact: "If ye then be risen with Christ." Given the fact of life-union with Jesus Christ, there are some key things to think about. Both imperatives, "seek" (v. 1) and "set your affections" (v. 2), involve thinking. Imperatives are always addressed to the will and identify what we are obliged to do.

First, *seek those things which are above.* The form of the verb demands a continuing and habitual process. This is not to be an occasional thought, but one that becomes regular routine. Furthermore, this seeking does not refer simply to an investigation, but includes the thoroughgoing effort to obtain what is sought. The direction of this ongoing effort is above, where Christ sits exalted in His session at the Father's right hand. This apostolic advice parallels the words of Christ Himself in His Sermon on the Mount, admonishing us to lay up treasures in heaven and not on earth because "where your treasure is, there will your heart be also" (Matt. 6:19–21). There is no treasure more valuable than Jesus, the pearl of great price. Nothing else approaches His infinite value and intrinsic worth. To regard Him so is to have our earthly hearts fixed there where He is and where we are in union with Him.

Again, this seeking is more than just an examination of the doctrine, but a striving to experience and possess the fullness of the blessing. Too often Christians are like the ten Israelite spies who admired and could describe the grapes of Canaan but failed to possess them; they remained on the border of blessing. Examining and expounding gospel truth is fundamental, but it is vital that we go beyond its exposition to its experience. We must live in the reality of what we believe. Let us not live on the border of spiritual blessing, but let us enter its fullness. Let us be like Caleb and Joshua, who entered into the possession of what God had promised and provided.

Second, *set your affection on things above*; literally, "be thinking about the above things." The form of this verb also demands continuing and habitual activity. Thinking is the exercise of the mind and is spiritually crucial. Paul uses the noun form cognate to our verb in Romans 8:6 when he says, "For to be carnally minded is death; but to be spiritually minded is life and peace." One's mind-set is a litmus test that reveals what one really is. Thinking is the first step to doing. Right thinking produces right behavior. It is imperative that the believer, therefore, habitually and routinely engage the mind on the above things, where Christ is and where the believer is with Christ in that throne-union.

I don't know how thinking works, but I know it works. I know that when you think about something hard enough and long enough, you can't stop thinking about it. I suppose the issue is what we think about when we're not thinking! Habitual thinking wears grooves in the brain. Check out Philippians 4:8, where Paul lists some of the above things to think about. We need "to groove our brains" with things that are true, honest, just, pure, lovely, of good report, virtuous, praiseworthy—all of which are subsumed in Christ Himself.

This obviously does not mean that we never think about other things, for other things are unavoidable parts of life. But it does mean that all we think about and all we do are governed by the fact that we are united to Christ. Thinking about that truth affects everything else. Contrary to the common adage that someone can be so heavenly minded as to be no earthly good, the gospel logic is that the more heavenly minded we become, the more earthly good we will be.

The Prospect of the Hidden Life
The prospect of the hidden life is that it will not remain hidden. A day is coming when faith will transition to sight, when the invisible will become visible, and when our subjective experience will become one with our objective position. The Greek verb translated "appear"

means to be manifest, completely revealed and open. Christ, "who is our life"—the essence of the life we possess and the object of our passions—will one day be openly revealed in all of His splendid glory. Adding to the wonder is the fact that we will be manifested in the same glory with Him. There is no separating Christ and His people, not then and not now.

The prospect of that certain glory shared with Christ puts all the stuff of time in its proper place. Occupation with Christ is the secret to everything in the Christian life. So living out our faith means that we live now with a view to then.

The Procedure: The Seen Life

What is true on the inside shows itself on the outside. Although our union with Christ is hidden from view, the evidences of that union should be seen. Doctrine breeds duty. Ethical demands flow from theological truths. Union with Christ looks like something.

In verses 5–17, the apostle details the implications of being in Christ, both in negative and positive terms. His logic was adopted by the Westminster divines in their classic definition of sanctification as "the work of God's free grace, whereby we are renewed in the whole man after the image of God, and are enabled more and more to die unto sin, and to live unto righteousness" (Shorter Catechism, Q. 35). We want to follow that logic as well as we consider what the hidden life is supposed to look like.

Death to Sin

In Colossians 3:5–11, the focus is on the negative component of this sanctification: death to sin. Believers are to put off the vices belonging to the old life outside of Christ. It only makes sense that if we died judicially to sin in union with Christ in His death on the cross, we should also die practically to sin as we live in union with His life in the resurrection. Here's how Paul puts it in Romans 6:4: "Therefore we are buried with him by baptism into death: that like as Christ was raised up from the dead by the glory of the Father, even so we also should walk in newness of life." Paul's imagery here is suggestive. In physical burial, the corrupting corpse is separated from the land of the living. In a remarkable irony, in this spiritual burial with

Christ, the "living" corpse of the believer is separated from the corruption of the world.

Paul's argument in verses 5–11 suggests three thoughts. First, he demands *the duty of death*. Paul issues commands; therefore, these are not simply apostolic or pastoral suggestions for optional behavior, but imperatives that demand obedience. We are to "mortify" our earthly "members" along with their sinful practices (v. 5). The word *members* usually designates physical limbs or body parts, but by metonymical extension it includes whatever is in us that is of this world that is bent to sin. It parallels what Paul calls the "old man," which we will consider in a moment.

In many ways, the biggest threat to our sanctification is self. Therefore, we must die to self. But this death is not by natural causes, for dying to self is most unnatural. The word *mortify*, perhaps, has lost some of its shock in modern usage. The word means to kill, with all of its violent connotations. This is suicide. We must kill self, put it to death. The language is blunt, forceful, and a bit shocking, but no more so than Christ's counsel to eliminate offending body parts for the spiritual welfare of the soul (Matt. 5:29–30). This member-killing refers to an urgent and immediate effort to eliminate by execution anything and everything that is at odds with God. If our life is truly in heaven, then we must kill off the sinful stuff of our earthly existence. The consequence of Christ's dying for us and our dying in Him is that we should not live anymore with a view to ourselves— our interests, ambitions, or desires that would be contrary to grace (see 2 Cor. 5:15).

We are also "to put off" sinful practices (Col. 3:8), those things that stain and thus ruin the appearance of a garment. The imagery changes, but the topic is the same. By using an illustration about changing clothes, Paul makes clear that life in Christ cannot look the same as before. It is only logical that after a bath, you would not put on the filthy clothes that made the bath necessary to begin with. So spiritually, after the washing of regeneration, we must put off the garments that have been mucked up from the dirt of this world. Life in union with Christ requires a visible transformation. The Bible knows nothing about a gospel that makes no demands on life or requires no changes. Grace finds sinners in the most indescribable of filth, but grace never leaves sinners where it finds them.

Second, Paul identifies *the sins subject to death*. He gives two extensive but not exhaustive lists of sins to illustrate the kind of behavior that is incongruous to the hidden life in Christ (vv. 5, 8). It is not my intent to define or elaborate on each of the specific vices, but I do want us to get the principal point the apostle is making.

Each group lists five sins, all of which relate to specific violations of the second division of God's Moral Law, the section dealing with man's relationship to man. Transgression of the second division is evidence of transgression against the first. Man's relationship with his fellows is a mirror of his relationship with God. In verse 5, the sins progress from outward acts to inward attitudes, whereas in verse 8, the sins move from inward attitudes to outward acts. Putting the two groups together creates a logical *chiasmus* in which the center focus is on the inward attitudes and thoughts.

Chiasmus is a common literary structure throughout the Bible. It's a different logic than modern Westerners are accustomed to using, but recognizing it often helps us follow the progression of a biblical argument. It is like a big X that draws attention to the point where the lines intersect.

So here, at the point of intersection, are the sins of the mind. This focus affirms our proposition that thinking determines behavior. Sins in the head are no less serious than sins of the hands.

Another literary technique is also operating when all ten sins are combined. It would be a mistake to assume that these specifically designated sins are the only ones with which we must be concerned. Paul employs a device called *brachylogy*, which is a partial list of something to indicate the totality of something. Paul's point, therefore, is not just that we should deal with these sins specifically, but with sin generally. He gives a representative list to include all vices that are contrary to holiness. The list of sins to which you may be particularly susceptible may differ from mine, but the text makes it clear that we must deal directly with the sins in our lives no matter what they are.

Verse 7 gives the hope that we can indeed mortify and put off our sins. There is power in the gospel to enable the transformation required by grace. The Colossian believers used to walk and live within the sphere of those sins, but now they don't. What used to characterize their lives no longer does. That reversal of lifestyle marks every genuine believer. No Christian is experientially as holy as he should be or as holy as he will be when he appears with Christ in glory, but neither is he as unholy as he was. Every saint can say with John Newton, "I am not what I ought to be…not what I wish to be…not what I hope to be…not what I once was…[but] 'by the grace of God I am what I am.'" (1 Cor. 15:10).[1]

Third, Paul explains *the reasons for death to sin*. He gives two reasons, one negative and one positive. Negatively, death to sin is necessary because sin angers God (v. 6). Every sin is a violation of His righteous justice, and His wrath is poised against it. Whereas the sinful world stands already condemned, all those in Christ have been delivered from condemnation (Rom. 8:1). Insomuch as Christians, then, are no longer under God's wrath, sinfulness should no longer be their practice. We are no longer subject to God's wrath because of Christ's atoning work. The cross stands as the greatest evidence of God's justice and wrath against sin. God put the cross of Christ in the place of our sins, and so must we. It was because of our sin that Christ died. To think of why He died and to remember that we died in union with Him is reason enough to die to sin.

Positively, death to sin is necessary because we have been restored to the image of God (Col. 3:9–10). Paul transitions to this argument by linking two causal participles ("put off" and "put on") to the imperative "lie not one to another," suggested by the imagery of dress. I don't think it is really true that clothes make the man, but they do reveal something about the man. I love to wear camouflage. So when I wear it along with a hat advertising Cabela's, you would be safe to assume that I hunt and that I wish I were in the woods, where neither you nor the deer could see me. On the other hand, if I were to wear the scrubs of a surgeon, that would be misleading and potentially dangerous if you believed what you saw. The point very simply is that you should dress according to what you are.

To be hidden in union with Christ demands death to sin because we have put off the old man and put on the new. John Calvin defines the "old man" as "whatever we bring from our mother's womb, and

---

1. Josiah Bull, *John Newton of Olney and St. Mary Woolnoth: An Autobiography and Narrative* (London: Religious Tract Society, 1870), 334.

whatever we are by nature."[2] In this context, it designates the unregenerate state in which there is no spiritual life or sensitivity and no impulse toward God or spiritual things. It is that nature that gives rise and expression to every evil deed.

The simple fact of the matter is that those who trust Christ don't wear those clothes anymore. No longer are they spiritually dead, insensitive, or motionless toward God. They look different because they have put on the new man.

The "new man" refers to that regenerate nature in which the Holy Spirit has implanted the principle of spiritual life. It is the new garment worn by everyone hidden in Christ. Paul describes the new man as being continually, habitually, progressively renewed in the knowledge of the Creator's image. It is not a sinless nature, but it wants to be and is headed in that direction.

It is beyond the scope of our meditation here to think about the full meaning and many implications of the image of God. Suffice it to say that it was the unique mark of man's original creation that was tragically marred by the fall of man into sin and wonderfully restored by God's grace through the gospel. Jesus Christ is the ideal image, even the perfect manifestation of God (1:15), and it is only through Him and in Him that we are being renewed. Christ, the Second Adam, reversed the curse and restored all lost by the first Adam.

So, regardless of race or nationality (3:11), every believer looks the same in this regard: they have all put on the new man. To wear the new man is to be adorned with Christ, who is all and in all: He is our uniform. Christ is everything in the realm of grace; there certainly is no experience or enjoyment of grace without Him. We die to sin by looking to Christ. As we look, we are changed progressively from glory to glory (2 Cor. 3:18) until He appears, when we will be like Him because we will see Him as He is (1 John 3:2). If seeing Christ with our eyes is how glorification works, it follows that seeing Christ with the eyes of faith is how sanctification works. There is something about seeing Jesus that makes us like Him.

---

2. John Calvin, *Commentaries on the Epistles of Paul the Apostle to the Philippians, Colossians, and Thessalonians*, trans. John Pringle (repr., Grand Rapids: Baker, 1999), 211, on Col. 3:9.

Alive to Righteousness

Living out our faith is more than not doing bad things; it involves doing good things as well. A life of faith is not just negative; it is most positive. Again, the Westminster Shorter Catechism says it well when it affirms that in our sanctification we are enabled "to live unto righteousness."

Paul concludes his argument about the "seen life" by expounding what it is to live spiritually (Col. 3:12–17). There are three points to his exposition. First, he delineates *the marks of spiritual life*. He continues the clothes analogy with the imperative "put on," and then lists the virtues that are to be seen in the new man, the style of clothing he is to wear. He addresses the imperative to those chosen by God, set apart as distinct, and the objects of fixed and continuing love—other ways of identifying those whose lives have been hidden with Christ in God.

Again, it is not my intent to define each of the virtues, all of which follow the same pattern as the list of vices by relating to the second division of the law. I want simply to draw some conclusions. Significantly, all of the virtues or marks are characteristics of Christ Himself. That should not be surprising, since Christlikeness is the ultimate objective of our salvation: God has predestinated us to be conformed to the image of His Son (Rom. 8:29). So to put on bowels of mercies is to be like Christ, and so it goes right down the list. Paul explicitly makes the connection when he sets Christ as the pattern for forgiveness: "as Christ forgave you, so also do ye" (Col. 3:13). It is noteworthy that Paul isolates love as the bond or belt that keeps everything complete and together (v. 14). The essence of this love is selflessness, and who more perfectly than Christ evidenced this selfless love to the climax of giving Himself for His church (Eph. 5:25)? Nothing will spoil, spot, and stain the Christian's wardrobe more than self. Be like Christ.

In this list of virtues Paul is employing the same literary device of brachylogy that he used to list the vices. These are random representative virtues that imply every conceivable virtue that conforms to and expresses obedience to God's standard of righteousness, His law, and His Son. Remember that what the world sees in us determines what it thinks of Christ. Ironically, as God sees us, the body, in

Christ, the Head, so the world sees Christ, the Head, through us, the body. That sobering thought should dictate our actions.

Second, Paul details *the method of spiritual life* (Col. 3:15–16). He issues three imperatives to explain how we are to live out our faith. All are in a form that expresses constant and habitual activity, underscoring the fact that living the Christian life is a fulltime occupation.

The first and third imperatives express tolerative ideas: "let the peace of God rule" (v. 15) and "let the word of Christ dwell" (v. 16). This is what should happen, and we should do what is necessary to allow it to happen. The peace that comes only from God must rule in our heart, our inner being where we think, feel, and determine to act. Although this peace could refer to the subjective peace of soul that comes from God evidenced by assurance of faith, confidence in forgiveness, and contentment, I'm more inclined to take it to be the objective peace of reconciliation that Christ accomplished through His blood (Col. 1:20). In a very real sense, the peace of God is summed up in Christ. That may account for the textual variant adopted in some versions that reads "the peace of Christ." So much in the text focuses on Christ's death and what we are to think about it that it makes sense that the reconciliation between God and us that Christ has enabled through His blood should also factor into our relationship to the body. The word *rule* is an athletic term meaning to act as an umpire, to arbitrate disputes, to make the calls. Peace with God translates to peace within the body of Christ. That happens when we allow Christ to settle every matter.

We should let the word about Christ (a topical genitive) dwell in us abundantly (3:16). To put it simply, the gospel should be at home in our hearts, where it then impacts every decision, plan, and activity of life. We are to live within the sphere of God's Word. For this to happen, we must know what Scripture says. *Sola Scriptura* is part of our Reformed tradition, but it must be more than just a component of our creed. Dwelling together implies intimacy, and if we confess love for the Word, it must be more than talk.

Paul uses a series of circumstantial participles to express what the indwelling Word looks like. First, it affects our conversation with fellow believers (teaching and admonishing one another). Second, it directs praise to God by causing us to sing in our hearts the new song that He has put there by grace by using psalms, hymns, and spiritual songs.

This, by the way, reflects a little different translation, involving only punctuation. As translated in the Authorized Version, psalms, hymns, and spiritual songs are the means of mutual teaching and admonition. I prefer translating the verse with a different punctuation, which more naturally links "with psalms and hymns and spiritual songs" to singing rather than teaching: "Let the word of Christ dwell in you richly, in all wisdom teaching and admonishing one another, with psalms and hymns and spiritual songs singing with grace in your heart to the Lord." But wherever the comma is placed, it is clear that the indwelling Word of Christ is going to be seen outwardly. That's our salient point for now. What is inside shows itself on the outside.

Sandwiched between the two tolerative imperatives is the command "be ye thankful" (v. 15). Constant and habitual gratitude is a key component of living out our faith. It is a common theme throughout Paul's letters and in his personal testimony. No exposition is required at this point. How can we not be thankful when we think of Christ, His work, and what that means for us personally?

Finally, Paul declares *the motive for spiritual life* (v. 17). Why we do what we do is important; motives matter. For the Christian, Christ's name and glory should be the principal concern in everything thought, said, and done. Scripture disallows the modern—or perhaps I should say postmodern—notion of compartmentalizing life so that religious life is somehow unrelated to everything else. On the contrary, nothing about life is outside the scope of the relationship we have with Jesus Christ. Who Christ is, His authority over us, our identification with Him, our knowledge of His will, and our thankfulness to God for Him all factor into every sphere of life. To say what we say and to do what we do consciously and intentionally in the name of Jesus unquestionably affects what we say and do. Right thinking produces right behavior. We can't get away from this axiom.

Living out our faith equates to simply living in the reality of the religion we say we believe. There can be no disconnect between belief and practice, between doctrine and duty. Objective truth must transfer to subjective experience. The more we know the gospel and our completeness in Christ, the more we can enjoy and experience the gospel in life. Theology is the most practical of disciplines and sciences. In the head, we must know the truth; in the heart, we must believe the truth; with the hands, we must implement and evidence the truth. Living our faith starts on the inside and shows itself on the outside.

CHAPTER 2

Living by the Spirit's Sanctifying Ministry

Ian Hamilton

Paul writes in Romans 8:12–14: "Therefore, brethren, we are debtors, not to the flesh, to live after the flesh. For if ye live after the flesh, ye shall die: but if ye through the Spirit do mortify the deeds of the body, ye shall live. For as many as are led by the Spirit of God, they are the sons of God."

Today, many Christians—even Reformed Christians—do not think as much about the Holy Trinity as Christians did in earlier ages. John Calvin, for example, wrote magnificently about the Trinity in Book One of his *Institutes of the Christian Religion*, citing a passage from Gregory of Nazianzus, a fourth-century Greek father, which, he said, "vastly delights me."[1] That passage about the Trinity is taken from one of Gregory's baptismal orations, where he said, "No sooner do I conceive of the One [member of the Trinity] than I am illumined by the splendor of the Three. No sooner do I distinguish them than I am carried back to the one. When I think of any one of the three I think of Him as the whole, and my eyes are filled, and the greater part of what I am thinking escapes me."[2]

Can you identify with Gregory of Nazianzus's words or with Calvin's delight in reading them? Can the church today identify with the love for the Holy Trinity that was so obvious in the early

---

1. John Calvin, *Institutes of the Christian Religion*, ed. John T. McNeill, trans. Ford Lewis Battles (Philadelphia: Westminster Press, 1960), 1.13.17.

2. Gregory Nazianzen, *Oration on Holy Baptism*, sec. 41, in *A Select Library of Nicene and Post-Nicene Fathers of the Christian Church, Second Series*, ed. Philip Schaff and Henry Wace (New York: The Christian Literature Co., 1894), 7:375.

church fathers and was replicated in the writings of Calvin, the other Reformers, and the Puritans?

What One Does, All Do

Let us begin to consider the work and ministry of the Holy Spirit by anchoring our thinking about the Spirit's sanctifying, beautifying work within the life and ministry of the Holy Trinity as a whole. A Latin phrase precisely captures what I am saying. It is *opera trinitatis ad extra indivisa sunt*, meaning "the works that are external to the Trinity are indivisible." What one does, all do. What one person does, the other persons do as well.

That does not mean that the Father and the Spirit died with the Son on Calvary's cross, but it does mean that through the eternal Spirit, our Savior, Jesus Christ, offered Himself to God the Father on the cross, as we read in Hebrews 9. Similarly, what the Holy Spirit does by way of eminency, as John Owen puts it, the Father and the Son also do.

Owen magnificently, movingly, and profoundly explains in Volume 2 of his *Collected Works* that, in the New Testament, love is almost always predicated of the Father; grace is almost always predicated of the Son; and comfort is almost always predicated of the Spirit. That does not mean the Lord Jesus Christ and the Spirit do not love, or that the Father and the Son do not comfort. But Owen gathers the testimony of Holy Scripture to help us understand that by way of eminency, the Father loves; by way of eminency, the Son pours out grace; and by way of eminency, the Spirit comforts.

Scripture tells us that the Spirit acts in the new covenant as the Spirit of the risen, reigning Jesus Christ, who was sent by Christ and His Father to apply the grace of Christ to the people of Christ. He does not act independently in His sanctifying, beautifying ministry, but is the agent by way of eminency of the Holy Trinity. What the Spirit does by way of eminency, the Father and the Son also do. They and their work are indivisible. When we think of one, we must then think of three. And when we think of the three, we must learn to understand the Trinitarian glory, the Trinitarian majesty, and the Trinitarian foundation of the Christian faith and of our personal union and communion with God in Christ by the bonding ministry of the Holy Spirit.

Conforming Us to Christ

Let us begin this study of the Holy Spirit by asking: *What precisely is the Spirit's sanctifying, beautifying ministry?* We will examine this question first in general terms, then look at it more specifically.

In general terms, the Holy Spirit indwells believers as the Spirit of Christ to make us like Christ. The great purpose of God concerning His people is to make us like His Son. The Holy Spirit is sent by God's predestined grand design to conform us to the image and likeness of the Son of God.

This is so that Christ might be the firstborn among many brothers, because God's ultimate purpose does not terminate in us but in Jesus Christ, who has ever been His beloved Son. Even when God the Father was cursing His Son on Calvary, He was surely saying, "If ever I loved Thee, My Jesus 'tis now." The great burden of the Father's heart is to exalt His Son by conforming the people of His Son to His likeness, to the praise and glory of God.

Because the Holy Spirit comes as the Spirit of Christ, Calvin may then argue that the chief title of the Holy Spirit in the New Testament in His new covenant ministry is "the Spirit of adoption." Paul thus says in verses 15 and 16: "For ye have not received the spirit of bondage again to fear; but ye have received the Spirit of adoption, whereby we cry, Abba, Father. The Spirit itself beareth witness with our spirit, that we are the children of God." In other words, the Holy Spirit has come as the Spirit of Christ, and because He is the Spirit of Christ, He is the Spirit of adoption.

What is more, He indwells us to remove all the hindrances, barriers, and impediments to our experience of entering into what he calls in verse 21 "the glorious liberty of the children of God." Nothing hinders us from enjoying the glorious privilege of our adoption more than the presence of indwelling sin in us. The Holy Spirit comes as the Spirit of adoption to put sin to death in our lives so that we might experience more radically, more gloriously, more personally, more deeply, and more effectively what it means to be children of the living God.

So, in general terms, that is what the Holy Spirit's sanctifying beautifying ministry is. Jesus Christ is the firstborn among many brothers. And by the Spirit of adoption, we have been brought into that community of faith, into the family of the living God. We have been engrafted into Christ, the firstborn One, and have received the Spirit of adoption, whereby we cry, "Abba, Father."

Enabling Us to Mortify Sin

But more particularly, what does the Holy Spirit, as the Spirit of Christ and of our adoption, actually do in our lives? What is His ongoing, new covenant ministry as the representative of the Holy Trinity?

Paul describes this ministry in verse 13, saying, "For if ye live after the flesh, ye shall die: but if ye through the Spirit do mortify the deeds of the body, ye shall live." This verse is often dislocated from its surrounding context. But note the words: "Ye shall live." In verse 14, Paul goes on to say, "For as many as are led by the Spirit of God, they are the sons of God." So what does it mean to be led by the Spirit of God? If only those who are led by the Spirit of God are the sons of God, how can they *not* be led by the Spirit of God?

That is a significant question. If we claim to be the sons of the living God, what credibility does our profession have? We might answer, "We are being led by the Spirit of God, and those who are led by the Spirit of God are the sons of God." But what is the distinguishing mark of the Spirit's leading that gives credibility to our profession that we truly are the sons of the living God? In verse 13, Paul says: "If ye live after the flesh, ye shall die: but if ye through the Spirit do mortify [put to death] the deeds of the body, ye shall live. For as many as are led by the Spirit of God" to mortify the deeds of the body, they shall live.

Thus, the distinguishing mark of the Holy Spirit's indwelling in us is that we, by the Spirit, are putting to death what Paul calls "the deeds of the body," or any sin that remains within us. By the grace of God, the atoning work of Christ, and the ministry of the Spirit, we who have believed in Christ have been set free from the guilt and power of sin. But the Lord has not yet set us free from every bit of the presence of sin. He thus gives us the Holy Spirit to help us remove everything in our lives that is not Jesus.

Greg Norman, a famous Australian golfer, was designing a golf course when he was asked, "What is in your mind when you look at this rough terrain and begin planning to create a golf course of it?" Norman said, "I look at the rough terrain and think, *I'll remove everything that isn't golf course.*" That is what the Holy Spirit does in us; He comes to remove everything that isn't Jesus from our lives. He comes to help us put to death the deeds of the body. Mortification of sin is the spiritual equivalent of uprooting and killing all of the weeds that threaten to overwhelm us and kill the flowers in our gardens. Without mortification, sin would overrun our lives and choke us to death.

Owen, the great Puritan writer, said: "Let not that man think he makes any progress in holiness who walks not over the bellies of his lusts. He who doth not kill sin in his way takes no steps towards his journey's end.... Be killing sin or it will be killing you."[3] Owen was stating in his own way what the apostle Paul tells us here: "If ye live after the flesh, ye shall die: but if ye through the Spirit do mortify the deeds of the body, ye shall live."

Paul makes at least three points in this statement. First, in saying, "ye shall live," he is telling us that the fullness of spiritual life, an ever-deepening fellowship with God, and the glorious liberty of the children of God are all impossible apart from mortification or putting sin to death in our bodies. As Owen wrote, "The vigour, and power, and comfort of our spiritual life depend on the mortification of the deeds of the flesh."[4]

Second, Paul is telling us that our usefulness to God and His church depends on our putting sin to death in our lives. He says, "But if ye through the Spirit do mortify the deeds of the body, ye shall live." In 2 Timothy 2:21, Paul says, "If a man therefore purge himself from these he shall be a vessel unto honour, sanctified, and meet for the master's use, and prepared unto every good work." If we purge ourselves from all that is dishonorable, sinful, and base, we shall be useful to the Master.

When Dan Edwards, a young theology student, was about to move to Germany, he received a letter from Robert Murray M'Cheyne, who was concerned that the young man might be affected by the infidelity that was beginning to raise its head within orthodox Christianity. M'Cheyne wrote: "Do not forget the culture of the inner man, I mean of the heart. How diligently the cavalry officer keeps his sabre clean and sharp. Every stain he rubs off with the greatest care. Remember, you are God's sword, His instrument. In great measure, according to

---

3. John Owen, *The Mortification of Sin in Believers,* in *The Works of John Owen* (repr., Edinburgh: Banner of Truth, 1965), 6:14, 9.

4. Owen, *The Mortification of Sin in Believers,* 6:9.

the purity and perfections of the instrument will be the success. It is not great talent God blesses so much as great likeness to Jesus."[5] The Holy Spirit comes to us to help us remove everything that isn't Jesus. Fullness of spiritual life and ever-deepening fellowship with God are impossible apart from mortification.

Third, Paul is reminding us that if we fail to mortify sin, we will cast a dark shadow over our profession to be children of God. Those who are led by the Spirit of God are the sons of God. If we are not led by the Spirit of God to put sin to death in our bodies, then our bodies will become the very instruments that sin uses to disseminate its heinousness, egregiousness, and wickedness.

Mortification does not earn us life in any way; only our Lord Jesus Christ does that. But mortification of sin is one thing we do that proves that our faith is alive. How can we claim to have a living, saving, uniting faith to Jesus Christ without day by day striving to kill the sin that once put our Savior to death?

Four Aspects of Mortification
Paul tells us four things about the Holy Spirit's beautifying, sanctifying discipline of mortification:

1. *Mortification is the believer's obligation.* Paul writes, "Therefore, brethren, we are debtors, not to the flesh, to live after the flesh. For if ye live after the flesh, ye shall die: but if ye through the Spirit do mortify the deeds of the body, ye shall live" (vv. 12–13). We are debtors to God, says Paul. We thus are obligated to God to put sin to death in our bodies. Paul also speaks of the believer as a debtor in 1:14—"I am debtor both to the Greeks, and to the Barbarians; both to the wise, and to the unwise." He is saying, in essence: "In order to preach to them, to proclaim to them, to make the gospel known to them, I have an obligation before God. I am a man who has received much, and therefore I must give much."

If you were to ask Paul, "Why do I have an obligation to put sin to death?" his answer might simply be, "the gospel." Mortification is our response to what the grace of God in Jesus Christ has done

---

5. Robert Murray M'Cheyne, Letter to Daniel Edwards, Oct. 2, 1840, in *Memoirs and Remains of the Rev. Robert Murray M'Cheyne*, ed. Andrew A. Bonar (Dundee: William Middleton, 1845), 243.

for us. We owe God everything. He has pardoned our sin. He has united us to His Son. By the grace of God in Jesus Christ, we are the bride of the Son of the Most High God. If our Savior died to put away sin, and if the Spirit has come into our lives to make us the dwelling place of God in the Spirit, then we have an obligation of gratitude to God to kill the sin that killed the Savior. It was for sin and sinners that Christ died.

Thomas Goodwin describes in a most remarkable way the particular and individual sins that were laid upon Christ by the Father. Goodwin may have been echoing Martin Luther's exposition of Galatians 3:13 in writing of the Father saying to the Son: "Be thou Peter that denyer; Paul that persecutor, blasphemer, and cruel oppressor; David that adulterer; that sinner that did eat the apple in paradise."[6] Goodwin was making the point that our sins in their "particularity" were laid on Christ. So when we are reminded of our particular sins, we must remember that it was those sins that killed our Savior and that our Savior atoned for all our particular sins.

If mortification is not rooted in the gospel, however, it becomes legalism at best and Romish superstition at worst. Only the gospel gives birth to true mortification. Owen wrote, "Not to be daily mortifying sin is to sin against the goodness, kindness, wisdom, grace, and love of God."[7]

Is mortification an evangelical obligation in your life? Do you find yourself a debtor to the grace of God that daily constrains you to put sin to death? Is this a grace and a duty that you daily seek to cultivate in your life? We have an obligation to do so.

2. *Mortification is the believer's responsibility.* Paul writes, "If ye live after the flesh, ye shall die: but if ye through the Spirit do mortify the deeds of the body, ye shall live." Unlike justification, which is an act of God's free grace, mortification involves our efforts. We are to put to death the misdeeds of the body. We know that we cannot begin to do that without the enabling help of the Holy Spirit. But Paul stresses here that this soul-purifying work demands our activity, not our passivity. We are never to let go and assume that God will do this work

---

6. Martin Luther, *Commentary on Saint Paul's Epistle to the Galatians* (New York: Robert Carter, 1844), 274–75.

7. Owen, *The Mortification of Sin in Believers*, 6:13.

for us, for God commands us to give ourselves to killing and rooting out this unwelcome, God-dishonoring, Christ-denying intruder in our lives. We are accountable for this. We are responsible before God.

3. Mortification is the believer's unceasing responsibility. Paul's verb tense here in verses 12–13 stresses that we are to keep on putting to death the deeds of the body. Mortification is not a once-for-all crisis experience; it is a daily and unceasing act. Our Lord Jesus Christ says in Luke 9:23, "If any man will come after me, let him deny himself, and take up his cross daily, and follow me." He did not excuse us from this ongoing work by saying, "You might be a fair-weather disciple or an immature disciple"; rather, the meaning of His words is clear: "If you do not take up your cross and nail yourself and all that you are to it every day, you cannot be My disciple."

That means that until the day we die, we are to wage war against sin in our lives. Sin "will no otherwise die," said Owen, "but by being gradually and constantly weakened; spare it, and it heals its wounds and recovers strength."[8] At times in your life, you might have thought: "Well, by the grace of God and by the goodness of His Spirit, I put that sin to death. I finally laid it in the dust." But soon after you ceased watching and praying about that sin, it began to rear its ugly head once again. Sanctification is a lifelong process; until you take your last breath, you must do battle against the world, the flesh, and the devil.

4. Mortification is carried out by the believer in dependence on the Spirit. "If ye through the Spirit do mortify the deeds of the body, ye shall live," says Paul. Any sin that remains in us has power. It has all the ingenuity of its master, Satan. We do not think enough about the malignant activity of Satan today. The Lord has given us the Holy Spirit to empower us to overcome any sin that remains within us, and the one who foments that remaining sin is Satan. Paul tells us in verse 26 that the Holy Spirit is our Helper. He is our *sunantilambane-tai*, Paul says. That very complex word tells us the following about the Spirit:

The Holy Spirit is our *Sun*; He is together with us, in cooperation with us. He is also *anti*; over and against us. He is together with us

---

8. Owen, *Pneumatologia: Or, A Discourse Concerning the Holy Spirit*, in *Works*, 3:545.

and yet over and against us. What is Paul saying? He is telling us that we are actively involved in our mortification, but also that every virtue we possess, every victory we win, and every thought we have of holiness also belong to Him, for it is the Spirit who enables us. The glory is His as the representative of the Holy Trinity. We must cast all of our victories at His feet because they are His victories, not ours.

How the Spirit Helps in Mortification

How does the Holy Spirit help us put sin to death? We know that the Holy Spirit, by God's grace, has tied us to Jesus Christ. He brings into our lives a new, God-centered nature, a new heart characterized by love for the Lord and a desire to please Him and keep His commandments. But as our Helper, He also enables us to put sin to death and mortify the deeds of the body. There are four ways in which the Spirit does this.

First, He shows us the loveliness of our Savior, Jesus Christ. Through the Holy Scriptures, He reveals to us the greatness, the majesty, the glory, the tenderness, the kindness, the power, and the holiness of Christ. In John 16:14, Jesus promised that when He gave His Spirit to believers, His Spirit would bring glory to Christ. The churches that are most animated by the Spirit are those that bring glory to Jesus Christ.

I live in Cambridge, which is the home of King's College. At night, if you walk through the campus, you can see its magnificent chapel, illuminated by lights. I have never seen anyone walk along King's Parade in Cambridge with his head down, looking at the floodlights and saying, "My, what wonderful wattage." Most people look up at what the light is illuminating.

That is what the Holy Spirit does. He shows us the loveliness of Christ, the multifaceted grace and glory of the Savior, and the excellence of His merited and personal grace. Like Joseph, we say, "When sin rears its ugly, egregious head, how could I do such a thing and sin against such a God?" (see Gen. 39:9). The Holy Spirit helps us see the loveliness of Jesus Christ.

Samuel Rutherford makes this beautiful response to his Savior: "O fair sun, and fair moon, and fair stars, and fair flowers, fair roses, and fair lilies, and fair creatures; but O ten thousand thousand times fairer Lord Jesus!"[9] The Spirit helps us to see how great Christ is and how tawdry and fleeting are the attractions of this world.

Second, the Spirit convinces us of the sinfulness of sin by showing us sin's true colors, its great deceitfulness, and its tragic end. He does this supremely through the Scriptures (Rom. 7:9–11), for the great function of the Holy Law of God is to bring us face to face with God. Goodwin said, "If thou wouldst see what sin is, go to Mount Calvary."[10] Notice that He said Mount Calvary, not Mount Sinai. The Spirit shows us what sin is by leading us through the Scriptures. The Spirit confronts us with the Holy Word of God and the holy standards of a holy God.

Sometimes He comes to us through the loving words of true friends. Think, for example, of David's response to the prophet Nathan's story about a man who had killed his neighbor's only sheep (see 2 Samuel 12). David says in Psalm 51:4, "Against thee, thee only, have I sinned, and done this evil in thy sight." We might object, saying: "David, get a grip on yourself. You have sinned against your wife, your children, and your nation. But against God? What do you mean by that?" David knew what he was saying, for the Holy Spirit had shown him the horrors of his sin. Yes, David had sinned against his wife, children, and nation, but most of all, he had sinned against God. The Spirit comes to us to graciously show us the sinfulness of the sin we commit against our loving God.

Third, the Spirit causes His graces to take root in our lives. Owen wrote: "Growing, thriving, and improving in universal holiness, is the great way of the mortification of sin.... The more we abound in the 'fruits of the Spirit,' the less shall we be concerned in the 'works of the flesh.'... This is that which will ruin sin, and without it nothing will contribute anything thereunto."[11] The Holy Spirit comes to plant the graces of Christ in our lives. He plants those graces in the inhospitable soil of our hearts where sin still lingers. As those graces are watered by the Word of God, by prayer, by the ministry of God's

---

9. Samuel Rutherford, "Letter to the Laird of Cally, 1637," in *Letters of Samuel Rutherford*, ed. Andrew A. Bonar (Edinburgh: Oliphant Anderson, 1891), 398.

10. Thomas Goodwin, *Christ the Mediator*, in *The Works of Thomas Goodwin* (repr., Grand Rapids: Reformation Heritage Books, 2006), 5:287.

11. Owen, *Pneumatologia*, 3:552–53.

people, and by the fellowship of the saints, they flourish and squeeze sin out of our lives.

Last, the Spirit gives us courage to put righteousness before sin in our lives. Think of Daniel, Peter, the apostles, and Luther; the Holy Spirit gave each of those men the courage to put truth before consequences and to resist compromise. The Holy Spirit helps us by giving us the grace we need to say no to certain people, certain places, certain television programs, certain literature, and certain Internet sites. But in all of this, the Spirit does not mortify sin without our cooperation. He blesses or prospers our striving, but He does not bless our sloth.

Let us remember that we are not engaged in an unequal battle against sin today, for the One who is in us is greater than the one who is in the world. No remaining sin in us is so ingrained or troublesome that we cannot kill it or mortify it with the Spirit's help.

In conclusion, consider these words from Owen regarding sanctification: "Set faith at work on Christ for the killing of thy sin…and thou wilt die a conqueror; yea, thou wilt, through the good providence of God, live to see thy lust dead at thy feet."[12] Put your faith in Christ, for He is the great sin-killer. Then, too, trust the Spirit of Christ, for He comes and says: "Child of God, we can do it together.

---

12. Owen, *Mortification of Sin in Believers*, 6:79.

CHAPTER 3

Living on Things Above: John Owen on Spiritual-Mindedness

John W. Tweeddale

Nestled just north of city-center London is a famous graveyard known as Bunhill Fields. The burial site is the resting place for many Puritan and nonconformist luminaries, such as John Bradford, John Bunyan, Isaac Watts, and John Owen. On Owen's tomb, there is a lengthy Latin inscription by Thomas Gilbert, "the common epitaph-maker for dissenters,"[1] that includes these words:

> In practical theology, he laid out before others the whole of the activity of the Holy Spirit, which he had first experienced in his own heart, according to the rule of the Word. And, leaving other things aside, he cultivated, and realised in practice, the blissful communion with God of which he wrote; a traveller (*viator*) on earth who grasped God like one in heaven.[2]

According to at least one of Owen's colleagues, he is best remembered as a pilgrim who traveled from this world to the next.[3] He was a man who lived his life on things above.

---

1. Anthony A. Wood, *Athenae Oxonienses: An Exact History of All the Writers and Bishops Who Have Had Their Education in the University of Oxford, to Which Are Added the Fasti, or Annals of the Said University*, vol. 5, ed. Philip Bliss (London, 1815), part 2, 180.

2. According to J. I. Packer, this translation is a "loose explanatory amplification" of the Latin. See J. I. Packer, *A Quest for Godliness: The Puritan Vision of the Christian Life* (Wheaton, Ill.: Crossway, 1990), 192, 350 n2; cf. Andrew Thomson, "Life of Dr Owen," in *The Works of John Owen*, 24 vols., ed. William H. Goold (London: Johnstone and Hunter, 1850), 1:cxiii–cxiv; Peter Toon, *God's Statesman: The Life and Work of John Owen* (Exeter: Paternoster Press, 1971), 182–83.

3. For the best overview on how Puritan theology was shaped by a pilgrim mentality, see Joel R. Beeke and Mark Jones, *A Puritan Theology: Doctrine for Life* (Grand

Evidence of Owen's pilgrim perspective can be gleaned from his dying words. On the morning of his death on August 24, 1683, Black Bartholomew's Day, his longtime friend William Payne came to his house to bid him farewell and bring him news that his final book, *The Glory of Christ*, was soon to be published. Payne said, "Doctor, I have just been putting your book on the Glory of Christ to the press." To which Owen memorably replied, "I am glad to hear that that performance is put to the press; but, O brother Payne, the long looked-for day is come at last, in which I shall see that glory in another manner than I have ever done yet, or was capable of doing in this world!"[4] Owen lived by faith in anticipation of seeing the glory of his Savior by sight.[5] He was a traveler on earth who grasped God like one in heaven.

For many, Owen is remembered only as a great theologian, but he is also known as an educational reformer, an advocate for toleration, and a defender of Protestant orthodoxy. His greatness as a theologian is tied directly to his pilgrim life. He wrote as one who enjoyed communion with the triune God. As Owen traveled up the mountain of biblical truth, he devoted his life to helping others see what he saw in the grandeur of God. A good example of this pilgrim perspective is found in one of his regrettably lesser-known works today, entitled *The Grace and Duty of Being Spiritually Minded.*[6]

Rapids: Reformation Heritage Books, 2012), 843–58. On Owen's pilgrim perspective within the context of Reformed scholasticism, see Sebastian Rehnman, *Divine Discourse: The Theological Methodology of John Owen* (Grand Rapids: Baker Academic, 2002), 68–71; Carl R. Trueman, *The Claims of Truth: John Owen's Trinitarian Theology* (Carlisle: Paternoster Press, 1998), 55–62; cf. Willem J. van Asselt, "The Fundamental Meaning of Theology: Archetypal and Ectypal Theology in Seventeenth-Century Reformed Thought," *Westminster Journal of Theology* 64 (2002): 319–35.

4. Toon, *God's Statesman*, 171.

5. Owen states, "There are two ways or degrees of beholding the glory of Christ which are constantly distinguished in the Scripture. The one is by faith, in this world,—which is 'the evidence of things not seen;' the other is by sight, or immediate vision in eternity, 2 Cor. v. 7, 'We walk by faith, and not be sight.' ...No man shall ever behold the glory of Christ by sight hereafter who doth not in some measure behold it by faith here in this world. Grace is a necessary preparation for glory, and faith for sight." Owen, *Meditations and Discourses on the Glory of Christ* (1684), in *Works*, 1:288.

6. For the best overviews of Owen's work on spiritual-mindedness, see Sinclair B. Ferguson, *John Owen on the Christian Life* (Edinburgh: Banner of Truth, 2001), 248–61; Derek W. H. Thomas, "John Owen and Spiritual-Mindedness: A Reflection on Reformed Spirituality," in *The Holy Spirit and Reformed Spirituality*, eds. Joel R.

Owen the Encourager

The book was published in 1681, just two years before Owen died, and thus represents some of his most mature thoughts on the Christian life. For this reason, one of his biographers states, "This is one of the most valuable and deservedly popular of all the Doctor's writings."[7]

According to Owen, the book was the result of his own "private meditations" during a time of acute illness, when he believed that he was not long for this world. He nevertheless regained some strength and decided to put his thoughts into sermon and print form for the benefit of his congregation at Leadenhall Street in London.[8] As Peter Toon explains, "This book (and others of this period) reveal that Owen's mind during his last few years of life were much taken up with meditation upon the Person of Christ, and of heaven."[9]

One of the unique features of this devotional work is that it reveals Owen's heart as a pilgrim-pastor. He taught others what he first preached to himself. In the words of William Orme: "When he enforces the grace and duty of spiritual-mindedness, he illustrates that which he daily loved and sought. His mouth spoke from the abundance of his heart, and that which he had tasted and felt himself, he was desirous of communicating to others."[10] Owen states in the preface to his book:

Beeke and Derek. W. H. Thomas (Grand Rapids: Reformation Heritage Books, 2013), 127–37. For evaluations of Owen's spirituality, with reference to this work, see also Philip Adair Craig, "The Bond of Grace and Duty in the Soteriology of John Owen: The Doctrine of Preparation for Grace and Glory as a Bulwark against Seventeenth-Century Anglo-American Antinomianism" (PhD dissertation, Trinity International University, 2005); John Hannah, "The Cure of Souls; or, Pastoral Counseling: The Insight of John Owen," *Reformation and Revival* 5.3 (1996): 71–92; Michael A. G. Haykin, *The Reformers and Puritans as Spiritual Mentors* (Ontario: Joshua Press, 2012), 125–42; Kelly M. Kapic, *Communion with God: The Divine and the Human in the Theology of John Owen* (Grand Rapids: Baker Academic, 2007); Timothy J. Keller, "Puritan Resources for Biblical Counseling," *The Journal of Pastoral Practice* 9.3 (1988): 11–44; David M. King, "The Affective Spirituality of John Owen," *Evangelical Quarterly* 68.3 (1996): 223–33; Packer, *A Quest for Godliness*, 191–218.

7. William Orme, *Memoirs of the Life, Writings, and Religious Connexions of John Owen* (London, 1820), 439.

8. Owen, *Works*, 7:263. The context of *Grace and Duty* is strikingly similar to his work on the glory of Christ mentioned above; see *Works*, 1:275. The two works in many ways should be read together.

9. Toon, *God's Statesman*, 168.

10. Orme, *Memoirs*, 462.

I acknowledge that these are the two things whereby I regulate my work in the whole course of my ministry. To impart those truths of whose power I hope I have had in some measure a real experience, and to press those duties [upon others] which present occasions, temptations, and other circumstances, do render necessary to be attended unto in a peculiar manner, are the things which I would principally apply myself unto in the work of teaching others; for as in the work of the ministry in general, the whole counsel of God concerning the salvation of the church by Jesus Christ is to be declared.[11]

Owen saw the whole course of his ministry as driven by two basic motivations: "zeal for God's glory and compassion for men's souls."[12] He knew that both the one who preaches and the ones who hear the message proclaimed will alike stand before the judgment seat of Christ. Therefore, Owen wanted to prepare both his heart and the hearts of his people for that day. His goal was to give them a "foretaste of glory."[13] For this reason, he wrote the book in order to train himself and his flock to set their minds and hearts on things above.

As William Goold explains, Owen penned his volume on spiritual-mindedness not so much as "a Boanerges [like the apostles James and John] set for the defence of the gospel, [but] as a Barnabas intent on the consolation of the saints."[14] In other words, here is Owen the encourager. Perhaps this is why the book was one of the favorites of the Scottish Presbyterian Thomas Chalmers. He states:

The following treatise of Dr Owen holds a distinguished rank among the voluminous writings of this celebrated author; and it is characterized by a forcible application of truth to the conscience—by a depth of experimental feeling—an accuracy of spiritual discernment into the intimacies and operations of the human mind—and a skill in exploring the secrecies of the heart, and the varieties of affection, and the ever-shifting phases of character,—which render this admirable Treastise...a valuable guide to the honest inquirer, in his scrutiny into the real state of his heart and affections.[15]

---

11. Owen, *Works*, 7:263.
12. Owen, *Works*, 7:263.
13. Owen, *Works*, 7:265.
14. William Goold, "Prefatory Note," in *Works*, 7:262.
15. Thomas Chalmers, "Introductory Essay," in John Owen, *The Grace and Duty of Being Spiritually Minded*, 2nd ed. (Glasgow: Printed for William Collins, 1826), xxi.

Having set the pilgrim context for this book, let's consider what Owen means by spiritual-mindedness.

Minding of the Spirit

The launching pad for Owen's book is his exposition of Romans 8:6: "For to be carnally minded is death; to be spiritually minded is life and peace." Building on the apostle Paul's argument in Romans 8, Owen contends that there are only two categories of people: the carnally minded and the spiritually minded. These two categories are antithetical to one another. As Owen states, "The difference between these two states is great, and the distance in a manner infinite, because an eternity in blessedness or misery doth depend upon it."[16] In short, the contrast between them is as stark as life and death.

Those who are ruled by the flesh are at enmity with God. Their fate is both spiritual and eternal death as the result of God's just punishment for rebellious thinking and living (see Eph. 2:1; Col. 2:13; Rom. 6:23; 8:13). In contrast, those who are ruled by the Holy Spirit enjoy life and peace, both in this life and the next. Even though the regenerate still battle against the flesh, they have a new principle of spiritual life that is at work in them (Gal. 5:17). As Christians, we are to no longer set our minds on carnal things but on spiritual things. Owen explains:

> The "minding of the Spirit" is the actual exercise of the mind as renewed by the Holy Ghost, as furnished with a principle of spiritual life and light, in its conception of spiritual things and the setting of its affections on them, as finding that relish and savour in them wherewith it is pleased and satisfied.[17]

The mind that was once set on carnal, fleshly, ungodly things now delights in, relishes, and savors spiritual things.

But what actually goes on when we think on spiritual things? According to Owen, the process of "minding" spiritual things includes three steps. First, there is the "actual exercise of the mind." This takes place when we fix our thoughts on the truths of God's Word and meditate on them day and night.[18]

---

16. Owen, *Works*, 7:268.
17. Owen, *Works*, 7:270.
18. Owen, *Works*, 7:270.

Second, Owen speaks of the "inclination, disposition, and frame of the mind, in all its affections."[19] Today we use the word *mind-set* to describe what Owen is articulating. The inclination of the mind refers to the process whereby, in our affections, we desire what we think upon. When you dwell on something long enough, your heart begins to cling to it. This idea is expressed in the phrase, "Absence makes the heart grow fonder." The more I think about my wife when I'm on a business trip, the more I desire to be with her. The point is that what we think about shapes and stirs our affections. According to Owen, the affections are the "palate of the soul" whereby we develop a taste for God.[20]

The third step is "complacency of mind." Owen calls this the "gust, relish, and savour" of thinking on spiritual things. When you think about something and it stirs your affections, you discover that the process of mulling over it brings you into a state of joy. For example, this is why we smile when we remember our wedding day, chuckle when we think about our children, or salivate when we daydream about a rib-eye steak. For Owen, "In this gust and relish lies the sweetness and satisfaction of spiritual life."[21] To the carnal mind, the truths of God's Word are bland, tasteless, and unappealing. For the Christian, however: "In this gust we taste by experience that God is gracious and that the love of Christ is better than wine, or whatever else hath the most grateful relish unto a sensual appetite. This is the proper foundation of that 'joy which is unspeakable and full of glory.'"[22] The love of Christ is insatiable. The more you experience His redeeming love, the more you desire it. The more you desire it, the more you want to dwell on it. The more you dwell on it, the more you cherish it and are satisfied by it. You can never "mind" Christ's love too often, since His love knows no bounds (see Eph. 3:14–21).

Based on his exegesis of Romans 8:6, Owen concludes this section by affirming two overarching principles that govern his entire discourse. First, "To be spiritually minded is the great distinguishing character of true believers from all unregenerate persons." Second,

19. Owen, *Works*, 7:270.
20. Owen, *Works*, 7:483.
21. Owen, *Works*, 7:270.
22. Owen, *Works*, 7:271.

"Where any are spiritually minded, there, and there alone, is life and peace."[23]

Progress in Spiritual-Mindedness

Owen's book is divided into two parts: chapters 1–10 focus on the exercise of the mind on spiritual things, and chapters 11–21 on the affections. Throughout, he explores the use of outward and ordinary means, such as preaching and prayer, in stirring the mind and shaping the affections. But first, Owen gives three rules or guidelines for evaluating progress in spiritual-mindedness.

The first rule is convicting: "Consider what proportion your thoughts on spiritual things bear" upon other things in your life.[24] In other words, to what extent am I seeking to glorify God in the grind of life in terms of vocation, family, and friendships? Our tendency is to prioritize material needs over spiritual truths. We fall into the trap of thinking that Sundays are for God while the rest of the week is for us. As Owen states, "The world will frequently make an inroad on the way to heaven, to disturb the passengers and wayfaring men."[25] Our high-stress, hyper-connected, fast-paced lives thrust us into lifestyle patterns that make it difficult for us to focus long on God. As a result, we attempt to fit Him in where we can. But God is not someone you fit into your schedule. Your schedule is made for Him. The bread you eat is devoured for Him. The beverage you drink is savored for Him. The clothes you purchase are worn for Him. The job you perform is done for Him. We don't live for things. We live for God. Owen raises an important question about our mind-set toward these "earthly affairs." We all live busy, distracted lives. Yet while "secular concernments" frequently (and understandably) impose themselves upon us "when we are engaged in spiritual duties," how often do spiritual thoughts "impose themselves on our minds while we are engaged in earthly affairs?"[26]

The second rule is challenging: "We should consider whether thoughts of spiritual things do constantly take possession of their proper seasons." Owen reflects on how we use organized and

---

23. Owen, *Works*, 7:271.
24. Owen, *Works*, 7:301.
25. Owen, *Works*, 7:304.
26. Owen, *Works*, 7:304, slightly edited.

discretionary time. He states: "There are some times and seasons in the course of men's lives wherein they retire themselves unto their own thoughts. The most busied men in the world have some times of thinking unto themselves."[27] He distinguishes between stated and spare seasons. Do you have stated, set-aside blocks of time for communion with God? How do you spend mornings and evenings when the rest of the household is in bed? Are you making the most of your daily exercise regimen, your commute to work, or that late-night bottle-feed? In the rhythm of everyday life, are you maximizing these moments to increase your affections for Christ? But perhaps a better indicator of your progress in spiritual-mindedness is how you spend unplanned spare time: "If we cannot afford unto God our spare time, it is evident that indeed we can afford nothing at all."[28] What do you think about when you have nothing else to think at all? Do you find your mind and heart drifting to the truths of God's Word? As Owen states:

> Ordinarily voluntary thoughts are the best measure and indication of the frame of our minds.... It is therefore evident that the predominancy of voluntary thoughts is the best and most sure indication of the inward frame and state of the mind.... Wherefore, to be spiritually minded is to have the course and stream of those thoughts which we ordinarily retreat unto, which we approve of as suited unto our affections, to be about spiritual things. Therein consists the minding of the Spirit.[29]

The third rule is comforting: "Consider how we are affected with our disappointments about these seasons."[30] In times of hurt and heartache, do you find yourself turning to Him who is a refuge for weary souls? Do you grieve over negligence in attending to spiritual things? The soul fixed on Christ will say: "How little have I been with Christ this day! How much time hath passed me without a thought of him! How foolish was I to be wanting to such or such an opportunity! I am in [debt] to myself, and have no rest until I be

---

27. Owen, *Works*, 7:305.
28. Owen, *Works*, 7:306.
29. Owen, *Works*, 7:275, 277.
30. Owen, *Works*, 7:306.

satisfied."[31] Even our mishaps in spiritual-mindedness have a way of driving us to Christ.

Means of Grace

What tools has God given to help us think more deeply and fully on spiritual things? Owen underscores the indispensability of the local church and the "outward means and occasions" that God has established for our spiritual growth.[32] In particular, he focuses on the divinely appointed means of preaching and prayer.[33] Spiritual-mindedness is demonstrated in a palpable love for the worship of God and a delight in the means that God has given for His worship. Owen states, "That all true believers, whose minds are spiritually renewed, have a singular delight in all the institutions and ordinances of divine worship is fully evident both in the examples of the saints in the Scripture and their own experience."[34]

Those who are spiritually minded do not delight simply in the external formalities of worship, such as the pleasure of going to church with friends and family, the splendor of God's people singing His praise, the comfort of prayer, the encouragement of hearing God's Word read and proclaimed, and the wonder of the sacraments. They revel in the fact that through these means God is known in Jesus Christ. Owen explains:

> What is it which believers do so delight in in the ordinances and institutions of divine gospel worship, and what is it that engageth their hearts and minds into a diligent observance of them, as also how and wherein they do exercise their love and delight? And I say, in general, that their delight in all ordinances of divine worship...is in Christ himself, or God in Christ. This alone is that which they seek after, cleave unto, and are satisfied withal. They make use of the streams, but only as means of communication with the spring. When men are really renewed in the spirit of their minds it is so. Their regard unto ordinances and duties of divine worship is, as they are appointed of God a blessed means of communion and intercourse between himself in Christ and their souls. By them doth Christ communicate of

31. Owen, *Works*, 7:307.
32. Owen, *Works*, 7:281.
33. Owen, *Works*, 7:282–98.
34. Owen, *Works*, 7:430.

his love and grace unto us; in and by them do we act faith and love on him.[35]

Faith in Christ is the key to experiencing lasting joy in worship. Without faith, our worship is cold and lifeless. Owen helpfully states, "Without the internal actings of the life of faith, external administrations of ordinances of worship are but dead things, nor can any believer obtain real satisfaction in them or refreshment by them without an inward experience of faith and love in them and by them."[36] There is a warning here against "cursed formality" in worship[37]—the ever-present temptation of only going through the motions. Owen especially cautions those whose "calling and work it is to study the Scripture...and yet may be, and oftentimes are, most remote from being spiritually minded."[38]

Spiritual-mindedness includes both the "internal actings of faith" and the "external administration of ordinances."[39] Neither can be neglected. In worship, we set our minds on Christ by faith as He is exhibited in God's Word preached, prayed, sung, and seen in the sacraments. Through these simple means, God grows our love and affection for Christ. Owen summarizes:

> This, therefore, is the first general spring of love of believers, of them whose affections are spiritually renewed, unto the ordinances of divine worship, and their delight in them: They have experience that in and by them their faith and love are excited unto a gracious exercise of themselves on God in Christ; and when they find it otherwise with them, they can have no rest in their souls.[40]

Life and Peace

Spiritual-mindedness is best cultivated within the context of the local church: "Believers, whose affections are spiritually renewed, do delight greatly in the duties of divine worship, because they are the great instituted way whereby they may give glory unto God."[41]

---

35. Owen, *Works*, 7:431–32.
36. Owen, *Works*, 7:435.
37. Owen, *Works*, 7:433.
38. Owen, *Works*, 7:276.
39. Owen, *Works*, 7:468–67.
40. Owen, *Works*, 7:433.
41. Owen, *Works*, 7:444.

Affections for Christ, however, wane when His Word and worship are disregarded. Where the means of grace have been abandoned, "men's religious affections have grown irregular, yea, wild and ungovernable."[42]

The pursuit of spiritual-mindedness demands both patience and perseverance, as progress at times can be disappointingly slow.[43] While distractions and discouragements may hinder growth for a season, the blessed hope of Romans 8:6 is that life and peace will accompany those who set their affections on things above, where Christ is (see Col. 3:1–3).[44] As sojourners on earth, our chief calling is to "think much of him who unto us is the life and centre of all the glory of heaven; that is Christ himself.... If we are spiritually minded, we should fix our thoughts on Christ above, as the centre of all heavenly glory."[45] The best way for you to do that is by placing yourself under the ministry of the Word in your local church.

---

42. Owen, *Works*, 7:469.
43. Owen, *Works*, 7:454.
44. Owen, *Works*, 7:495–97.
45. Owen, *Works*, 7:344, cf. 420.

CHAPTER 4

Living by the Means of Grace: How God Beautifies His Children

Ian Hamilton

God's ultimate purpose concerns the glory of His Son, not the beautifying of His children. God is intent on beautifying His redeemed children, but this is His proximate, not ultimate, purpose. God's ultimate purpose is to conform His children to the likeness of His Son *in order* to make Him "the firstborn among many brethren" (Rom. 8:29). The heavenly Father's first priority does not terminate on you or me, but on His beloved Son.

God's Beautifying Template
Romans 8:29 makes it absolutely clear that Jesus Christ is the essence, the epitome, and the ultimate paradigm of the beauty to which God seeks to conform all His children. He alone is "altogether lovely" (Song 5:16). I need hardly tell you that the Savior's beauty is preeminently moral and spiritual, not physical. At the very moment that "he [had] no form nor comeliness…no beauty that we should desire him" (Isa. 53:2), He was "altogether lovely." The beauty of the Savior that pervaded and shone through His humanity was nothing less than the moral glory of God. When the Lord brings us to the new birth, the birth from above, He plants within our yet sinful lives "his seed" (1 John 3:9), what Henry Scougal famously called "The life of God in the soul of man." God's purpose in saving sinners is not only to save them but to sanctify them, to transform them into the likeness of His Son.

Colossians 3:12–16 is a magnificent and deeply humbling portrait of the child of God:

Put on therefore, as the elect of God, holy and beloved, bowels of mercies, kindness, humbleness of mind, meekness, longsuffering; forbearing one another, and forgiving one another, if any man have a quarrel against any: even as Christ forgave you, so also do ye. And above all these things put on charity, which is the bond of perfectness. And let the peace of God rule in your hearts, to the which also ye are called in one body; and be ye thankful. Let the word of Christ dwell in you richly in all wisdom; teaching and admonishing one another in psalms and hymns and spiritual songs, singing with grace in your hearts to the Lord.

This is Jesus, the perfect, elect Servant-Son of the Father. This is what the elect of God are to look like. Is this what you look like? Is this what your church or my church looks like? What power and credibility such beauty would give to our evangelism!

It is God's ultimate purpose to exalt His Son and to make all His blood-bought, redeemed children like His Son, to conform us to the beauty of His likeness. But how does God go about the work of conforming us to the likeness of His Son, of "beautifying His children"?

What God Does Not Do

We need first to be absolutely clear that there is no one experience, no matter how deep, profound, and transformative, that perfectly beautifies God's children. We must learn instinctively to avoid like the plague all "second-blessing" theologies and experiences. Every Christian is summoned to "grow in grace and in the knowledge of our Lord and Saviour Jesus Christ" (2 Peter 3:18). I wonder whether Peter had in his mind Luke 2:40, 52? Our Savior's growth, of course, was not from imperfection to perfection, but from one degree of glory to another (Heb. 5:8). But our growth is from imperfection to perfection, though we will not attain perfection until our lowly bodies are transformed to be like Christ's glorious body at His coming (Phil. 3:20–21). Christian beauty, likeness to Christ, doesn't just "happen" (cf. v. 13). Paul applied himself with relentless, single-minded determination to "the prize of the high calling of God in Christ Jesus" (v. 14). Paul was a "one thing I do" man (v. 13). Are you a "one thing I do" man or woman? Is it your daily resolve to grow in the grace and knowledge of the Lord Jesus Christ? It will not just happen. Peter exhorts us to give all diligence to add to our faith (2 Peter 1:5), and

Paul summons us to work out our own salvation with fear and trembling, always knowing that it is God who works in us both to will and to do of His good pleasure (Phil. 2:12–13).

How, Then, Does God Beautify His Children?

God beautifies His children supremely, but not only by the "ordinary means of grace" (which are actually "extraordinary"). Why do I say "supremely, but not only"? For this reason: God works *all things* together for the good of His children (Rom. 8:28). God presses all of life into His service as means of grace. I am conscious that our Reformation heritage has stressed, and rightly so, the "ordinary means of grace": the preaching, hearing, and reading of God's Word, the sacraments of baptism and the Lord's Supper, corporate and private prayer, and godly discipline. But there is a danger to avoid here, the danger of thinking that growth in grace is tied to those formally ordained means of grace. In Romans 8:28, we are reminded that "all things" are means of grace to God's children as He wisely, sovereignly, gloriously, and mysteriously bends them to the beautifying of His children.

There is an ocean of encouragement for us in these words. All of life is bent by God, shaped by God, and invaded by God to secure the good of His people. God's sovereign providence is one of the great anchors that supports and keeps the souls of believers. Anchors do not keep you from being buffeted and battered by storms, but they do keep you from being swept off course! Every incident and circumstance in life can be a means of grace in the kind providence of God as we submit to and embrace His ever-wise purposes. God is personally and actively involved in every detail of His children's lives, pursuing the holiness of His people. Your growth in grace is not tied to those occasions when you corporately and consciously engage in the Word, the sacraments, and prayer. In "all things," God works for the good of those who love Him, those who are called according to His purpose.

The Fellowship of the Church

More particularly, however, the principal and principial context of the means of grace is the fellowship of the saints, the church of God.

In an age of unbridled individualism among evangelical Christians, we need to be reminded again and again of the centrality and importance of the church in the economy of God. We are so unconsciously infected by the incipient and strident individualism of the age that many Christians no longer instinctively think in corporate and covenantal terms (cf. Eph. 3:19). The church is the supreme (if not the only) context in which the means of grace operate. Working through the Spirit and by His Word, God uses the means of grace for the gathering in of His elect and their subsequent edification and sanctification. To this end, the risen Lord has endowed His church with all kinds of spiritual gifts and given to it offices or ministries for the preaching of the Word, the administration of the sacraments, and the exercise of godly discipline "for the perfecting of the saints" (Eph. 4:7–13).

Paul is highlighting the truth that the church, the local covenant fellowship, is the supreme locus for the exposition of those gifts that are means of grace.

The significance of the church with respect to the sanctifying of the elect was a dominant theme in the writings of the magisterial Reformers. Listen to John Calvin as he begins his exposition of the church: "I shall start, then, with the church, into whose bosom God is pleased to gather his sons, not only that they may be nourished by her help and ministry...but also that they may be guided by her motherly care until they mature and at last reach the goal of faith... so that, for those to whom he [God] is Father the church may also be Mother."[1]

In his commentary on Ephesians 4:12, Calvin makes the same point: "The church is the common mother of all the godly, which bears, nourishes, and brings up children in the Lord, kings and peasants alike; and this is done by the ministry."[2]

---

1. John Calvin, *Institutes of the Christian Religion*, Library of Christian Classics, vols. XX–XXI, ed. John T. McNeill, trans. Ford Lewis Battles (Philadelphia: The Westminster Press 1960), 4.1.1. Calvin is, of course, consciously echoing Cyprian: "You cannot have God for your Father unless you have the church for your Mother" (*On the Unity of the Catholic Church*, vi). The Reformers were more than happy to endorse, rightly understood, the Patristic aphorism, "*Extra ecclesiam nulla salus*" (outside the church there is no salvation)!

2. John Calvin, *Commentaries on the Epistles of Paul to the Galatians and Ephesians*, trans. William Pringle (repr., Grand Rapids: Baker, 1999), 282, on Eph. 4:12.

Calvin is simply echoing the teaching of God's Word. The great means of grace are located within the fellowship and ministry of Christ's church. Calvin doesn't mean, and I don't mean, that Christians should not cultivate individual and familial communion with God. But do we give to the church the place it ought to have in our lives? Are we devoted to its fellowship? Its ministry? Its purity? Its God-ordained centrality? Are you like the psalmist who said, "I was glad when they said unto me, 'Let us go into the house of the LORD'" (Ps. 122:1)?

This corporate, covenantal note was imbedded in the life of Christ's church from the beginning. It was a striking feature of old covenant religion. It was a striking feature at the inception of new covenant religion (Acts 2:42). The fellowship of the saints, God's church, was prized and cherished. The early Christians "continued steadfastly" in the "fellowship." The church was the people of God, it was the "holy temple," in which "the Spirit of God dwelleth" (Eph. 2:21–22; 1 Cor. 3:16–17). This basic yet deeply profound biblical truth not only honors the one institution established by our Lord Jesus Christ, it also helps us to resist the atomizing, fragmenting mind-set that so bedevils evangelical Christianity in this present age. Reformation Christianity not only magnified the justifying grace and imputed righteousness that becomes the possession of every believing sinner, it labored to set that justifying grace in its biblical context, that is to say, its corporate and covenantal context. Justifying grace not only brings you into saving union with Christ, it brings you into the fellowship of His body, the church.

The Beautifying Ministry of the Word of God
It is a Reformed truism that God's usual, if not invariable, means for beautifying His children is the ministry of His living, powerful, wise, good, and infallible Word. It is the Word preached, made visible in the sacraments, applied to the life of the church, and voiced in Spirit-inspired prayer that the Holy Spirit uses to make us more like our Lord Jesus Christ. More particularly, what the Holy Spirit first produced in Christ He comes in His new covenant ministry to reproduce in the people of Christ. This is what Calvin called the Spirit's ministry of "replication."

To appreciate the Spirit's sanctifying ministry in believers through the Word, we need first to appreciate His sanctifying ministry in Christ through the Word.

Jesus and the Word of God

The New Testament tells us that our Lord's sanctification was both definitive and progressive. We read in Luke 1:35, "The Holy Ghost shall come upon thee, and the power of the Highest shall overshadow thee: therefore also that holy thing which shall be born of thee shall be called the Son of God." From His mother's womb, as no other, Jesus was "holy, harmless, undefiled, separate from sinners" (Heb. 7:26). But Luke also tells us that "Jesus increased in wisdom and stature, and in favour with God and man" (2:52). He "increased in wisdom," just as He "learned...obedience...being made perfect" (Heb. 5:8–9).

But how did Jesus increase in wisdom, learn obedience, and become perfect? The Bible's answer is clear: through living under the Word of God (cf. Isa. 50:4–5). As the Lord's Servant, Jesus lived "under the Word." He describes Himself here as a Servant who was taught: "Morning by morning, he wakeneth mine ear to hear as the learned [as 'one who is taught']." The Lord God opened His ear. And because He has been taught, He knows "how to speak a word in season to him that is weary." Notice, "The Lord GOD hath opened mine ear." As the Servant of the Lord, our covenant Head in our frail flesh, He needed the Lord to open His ears to hear! The Word of God was absolutely instrumental in the developing sanctification of our Lord Jesus.

When Jesus was tempted by the devil, what did He do (cf. Luke 4:4, 8, 12)? Three times Jesus brought to mind words, pertinent and powerful words, from Deuteronomy 8:3, 6:13, and 6:16. How was He able to do this? How did Jesus acquire this knowledge of the Word of God? Was it immediately and indelibly impressed on His DNA while He was in the womb? If so, then His humanity is not our humanity! The human nature He took to Himself was not created *ex nihilo*, but was inherited through Mary. It was our human nature, "addicted to so many wretchednesses," as Calvin so vividly puts it, that the Savior took to Himself—notwithstanding His sinlessness.[3] No, just as He "learned obedience," so He learned the Word of God. His mind and heart were so saturated with the Word of God that He was able immediately to bring that Word to mind and repulse the devil's temptations.

Here is the key thing: what the Spirit first produced in Christ, He comes by His ministry of replication to produce in His people.

The Christian and the Word of God

Consider three texts:

John 17:17: "Sanctify them through thy truth: thy word is truth." Jesus is praying that His Father's truth, His living Word, will shape and sanctify His disciples. But as Robert Dabney comments, "Truth has no adequate efficiency to sanctify by itself...yet it has a natural adaptation to be the means of sanctification in the hands of the Holy Ghost."[4]

Psalm 119:11: "Thy word have I hid in mine heart, that I might not sin against thee." The psalmist could hardly be saying that the mere remembrance of God's Word, in its syllables and syntax, could keep him from sin. It is that Word applied and blessed to us by the mortifying and vivifying ministry of the Holy Spirit that keeps us from sin.

Psalm 119:18: "Open thou mine eyes, that I may behold wondrous things out of thy law." Here we see two things:

First, we see the psalmist's faith. Every exercise in the believer's life is to be an exercise of faith. The psalmist is acknowledging his dependence on the covenant Lord to give him true understanding, and he does so as a believer! When God makes us new creations in Christ, He does not plant within us a lifetime of unaided understanding. Rather, He gives us His Holy Spirit, the Spirit of the risen, exalted Jesus Christ, and He would have us come to Him day by day in believing dependence, just as the Savior did in the frailty of our flesh!

---

3. John Calvin, *The Gospel according to St John 1–10*, trans. T. H. L. Parker, Calvin's Commentaries, ed. David W. Torrance and Thomas F. Torrance (Grand Rapids: Eerdmans, 1961), 20, on John 1:14.

4. Robert Dabney, *Lectures in Systematic Theology* (Grand Rapids: Zondervan, 1972), 665.

Second, we see the psalmist's humility. He does not content himself with his standing before God, with his past insights, or with his divinely appointed office. He comes to the Word of God in a spirit of personal humility before God. The psalmist's divine giftedness is no assurance that he is able to understand the mind of God!

John Owen, the English Puritan pastor-theologian, put the matter memorably: "He that would utterly separate the Spirit from the word had as good burn his Bible. The bare letter of the NT will no more ingenerate faith and obedience in the souls of men...than the letter of the OT doth so at this day among the Jews."[5] He makes the same point in his famous work on mortification: "All ways and means without [the Holy Ghost] are as a thing of naught."[6] Owen is saying only what the Word of God itself says (cf. 1 Cor. 2:9–12). If I were given a book on advanced calculus, I would know the book was about calculus (I can read!). I could even at one time make a little sense of elementary integration and differentiation. But the internal coherence of the book, its fundamental premises, its considered conclusions, and its remarkable applications to life would all escape me. I need someone who understands calculus from the inside to explain it to me (cf. Acts 8:30–38).

The sanctifying work of God comes to us by His Word and Spirit, through faith. Wilhelmus à Brakel, the experiential Dutch theologian, wrote:

> It is there [in the Word of God] that sins are set forth in their abominable nature and spiritual life is revealed in its desirability. Scripture convicts, rebukes, threatens, and judges. It contains exhortations and various inducements. Christ is presented as the fountain of sanctification, and it contains the promises. All this the Holy Spirit applies to the hearts of believers, exercising and activating them unto sanctification—the Word of God being the instrument in the hand of God (apart from which a means cannot be operative).[7]

---

5. John Owen, *The Works of John Owen* (Edinburgh: Banner of Truth, 1965), 3:192–93.

6. Owen, *Works*, 6.41.

7. Wilhelmus à Brakel, *The Christian's Reasonable Service* (Grand Rapids: Reformation Heritage Books, 1994), 3.5.

The Beautifying Ministry of the Sacraments

Calvin said that the Lord gave us His sacraments "to sustain the weakness of our faith."[8] The sacraments are divine accommodations to our sinful weakness. In a wonderfully vivid and beautifully written passage, Calvin says:

> But as our faith is slight and feeble unless it be propped up on all sides and sustained by every means, it trembles, wavers, totters, and at last gives way. Here our merciful Lord, according to His infinite kindness, so tempers Himself to our capacity that, since we are creatures who always creep on the ground, cleave to the flesh, and, do not think about or conceive of anything spiritual, He condescends to lead us to Himself even by these earthly elements, and to set before us in the flesh a mirror of spiritual blessings.[9]

While this is no doubt true, it is surely no less true that the sacraments are also adapted to our humanity *per se*. Calvin himself seems to acknowledge this. Quoting Chrysostom, he recognizes that it is "because we have souls engrafted in bodies [that] he imparts spiritual things under visible ones."[10] This suggests that the sacraments are not merely gracious "accommodations" to our sinful capacities; more properly, perhaps, they are gracious accommodations to our intrinsic humanity just as in the garden of Eden, the Lord gave Adam a tree to confirm and make visible to him His promise (and threat).

There is little space left to consider the beautifying ministry of prayer and church discipline. What must be said, however, is that prayer and church discipline are not independent of God's Word; rather, they are informed and shaped by God's Word.

The Beautifying Ministry of Prayer

It is a fact of history that the most Christlike Christians are the most prayerful Christians. Why should that be? For this simple reason: you become like the people you live with and love! Have you not noticed that? Prayer is communion with God. It is a spiritual grace.

The early chapters of Acts reveal God's people constantly at prayer: "These all continued with one accord in prayer.... They

---

8. Calvin, *Institutes*, 4.14.1.
9. Calvin, *Institutes*, 4.14.3.
10. Calvin, *Institutes*, 4.14.3.

continued stedfastly…in prayers…. They lifted up their voice to God with one accord, and said, Lord, thou art God" (Acts 1:14; 2:42; 4:24). Prayer was fundamental, not marginal; it was central, not supplemental, to the life of the early church. Was it not this heartfelt sense of their dependence on God that gave such luster to the witness of these early believers?

Throughout his letters, Paul enjoins the churches to pray, not as a mere formal spiritual exercise, but as the mark of their sense of creaturely dependence on the grace and sovereign power of God. More than anything else, the example of our Lord Jesus should impress on us the sanctifying power of prayer. He lived a life of prayer. He taught His disciples to pray. He commanded all God's people to pray (Matt. 7:7–11). The pulsebeat of His life was prayerful dependence on His Father and the enabling of the Holy Spirit.

In prayer, and as our prayers are informed by God's Word, our desires become aligned with God's desires. His thoughts become our thoughts. In this way, likeness to the Savior becomes an ever-developing feature of our lives.

The Beautifying Ministry of Church Discipline

It may seem strange to some people that church discipline could ever contribute to the beautifying of God's children, but in the hands of the Holy Spirit, ministered with grace, and received in humility, it does. Church discipline is commanded by God in His Word and is to reflect His discipline of His children: "whom the Lord loveth he chasteneth, and scourgeth every son whom he receiveth" (Heb. 12:6, quoting Prov. 3:12). And why does the Lord do this? "That we might be partakers of his holiness" and yield "the peaceable fruit of righteousness" (Heb. 12:10, 11).

Some years ago, the elders in my congregation interviewed a young student for membership. When asked why she wanted to be a member of Cambridge Presbyterian Church, she replied, "I was present when the church disciplined a woman for ungodly behavior, and I thought I wanted to belong to a church that took the honor of God that seriously." I and my fellow elders were speechless with thankfulness to God.

Yes, church discipline can be, and sadly has been, exercised harshly and clinically. But when exercised in love, under the clear teaching of God's Word, its purpose is to humble backslidden believers and bring the church into a new sense of the lovingkindness, holiness, and tender mercy of God.

Are you living by the means of grace? There are no shortcuts to godliness, to the likeness of Christ, who is the essence and epitome of godliness. Use all the ordained means God has given to you. Cherish every opportunity to gather with God's people. Prize the unity and peace of Christ's church, the soil that nourishes the means of grace. Resist the temptation to separate yourself from the church because of its failures. God is longsuffering toward His church, and we are called to be imitators of God.

CHRISTIAN LIVING IN ITS
HUMAN BRANCHES

CHAPTER 5

Living in the Family:
Thoughts from William Gouge

Joel R. Beeke

A family is a little church and a little nation.
—WILLIAM GOUGE[1]

There are few better examples of the beauty and glory of Christian living and of Reformed Christianity in action than the lives of the Puritans at home. Their views on marriage and family life were biblical, positive, and lavish. J. I. Packer writes that the Puritans were "the creators of the English Christian marriage, the English Christian family and the English Christian home."[2] For the Puritans, marriage was sacred because it was a covenant instituted by God Himself (Mal. 2:14). Edmund Morgan summarizes their view:

> Every proper marriage since the first was founded on a covenant to which the free and voluntary consent of both parties was necessary.... Since time began no man and woman had ever been allowed to fix the terms upon which they would agree to be husband and wife. God had established the rules of marriage when he solemnized the first one, and he had made no changes in them since then. The covenant of marriage was a promise to obey those rules without conditions and without reservations.[3]

---

1. William Gouge, *Building a Godly Home, Vol. 1, A Holy Vision for Family Life*, ed. Scott Brown and Joel R. Beeke (Grand Rapids: Reformation Heritage Books, 2013), 20. Parts of this chapter are drawn from my *Living for God's Glory: An Introduction to Calvinism* (Lake Mary, Fla.: Reformation Trust, 2008), 317–48. Heartfelt thanks to Paul Smalley for his research assistance.

2. J. I. Packer, *A Quest for Godliness: The Puritan Vision of the Christian Life* (Wheaton, Ill.: Crossway, 1994), 341–42.

3. Edmund Morgan, *The Puritan Family: Religion and Domestic Relations in Seventeenth-Century New England* (New York: Harper & Row, 1966), 30.

The Puritans have bequeathed to us the biblical concept of a well-ordered, happy Christian home, where love abounds between husband and wife, and parents and children. Their writings[4] reveal this outlook, and many scholars have confirmed it through the years.[5] Their biblical vision for the home is sorely needed in our day

---

4. Richard Adams, "What are the Duties of Parents and Children; and how are they to be Managed According to Scripture?" *Puritan Sermons 1659–1689* (Wheaton, Ill: Richard Owen Roberts, 1981), 2:303–58; Isaac Ambrose, *Works of Isaac Ambrose* (London: Thomas Tegg & Son, 1872); Richard Baxter, "The Poor Man's Family Book," in *The Practical Works of Richard Baxter* (Morgan, Pa.: Soli Deo Gloria, 1996), 4:165–289; Paul Bayne, *An Entire Commentary upon the Whole Epistle of St. Paul to the Ephesians* (Edinburgh: James Nichol, 1866), 491–563; Robert Bolton, *General Directions for a Comfortable Walking with God* (Morgan, Pa.: Soli Deo Gloria, 1995), 262–81; Thomas Boston, "Duties of Husband and Wife; Sermon XXIII," in *The Works of Thomas Boston*, ed. Samuel M'Millan (Wheaton, Ill: Richard Owen Roberts, 1980), 4:209–18; John Bunyan, "Family Duty," *Free Grace Broadcaster*, no. 170 (1999): 15–28; John Cotton, *A Meet Help: Or, a Wedding Sermon* (Boston: B. Green & J. Allen, 1699); John Dod and Robert Cleaver, *A Godly Form of Household Government* (London: Thomas Man, 1598); Thomas Doolittle, "How May the Duty of Daily Family Prayer be Best Managed for the Spiritual Benefit of Every One in the Family?" in *Puritan Sermons, 1659–1689* (reprint, Wheaton, Ill.: Richard Owen Roberts, 1981), 2:194–272; Thomas Gataker, "A Good Wife God's Gift," "A Wife in Deed," and "Marriage Duties," in *Certain Sermons* (London: John Haviland, 1637); Thomas Gataker, *A Marriage Prayer* (London: John Haviland, 1624), 134–208; William Gouge, *Of Domestical Duties* (Pensacola: Puritan Reprints, 2006); Matthew Griffith, *Bethel: or, a Form for Families* (London: Richard Badger, 1633); George Hamond, *The Case for Family Worship* (Orlando: Soli Deo Gloria, 2005); Matthew Henry, "A Church in the House," in *Complete Works of Matthew Henry* (Grand Rapids: Baker, 1978), 1:248–67; William Perkins, "Christian Oeconomy," in *The Works of William Perkins*, ed. Ian Breward (Appleford, England: Sutton Courtenay Press, 1970), 416–39; John Robinson, *The Works of John Robinson*, vol. 3 (Boston: Doctrinal Tract and Book Society, 1851); Daniel Rogers, *Matrimonial Honour* (London: Th. Harper, 1642); Henry Scudder, *The Godly Man's Choice* (London: Matthew Simmons for Henry Overton, 1644); Henry Smith, "A Preparative to Marriage," in *The Works of Henry Smith* (Stoke-on-Trent, England: Tentmaker Publications, 2002), 1:5–40; William Whately, *A Bride-Bush or A Wedding Sermon* (Norwood, N.J.: Walter J. Johnson, 1975); and William Whately, *A Care-Cloth or the Cumbers and Troubles of Marriage* (Norwood, N.J.: Walter J. Johnson, 1975).

5. J. Philip Arthur, "The Puritan Family," *The Answer of a Good Conscience*, Westminster Conference, 1997 (London: n.p., 1998), 75–94; Lawrence J. Bilkes, "The Scriptural Puritan Marriage" (unpublished paper for Puritan theology class at Puritan Reformed Theological Seminary, Grand Rapids, 2002); E. Braund, "Daily Life Among the Puritans," *The Puritan Papers: Vol. One*, ed. J. I. Packer (Phillipsburg, N.J.: P&R, 2000), 155–66; Francis J. Bremer, *The Puritan Experiment: New England Society from Bradford to Edwards* (New York: St. Martin's Press, n.d.), 176–80; Catherine A. Brekus, "Children of Wrath, Children of Grace: Jonathan Edwards

of self-gratification and disrespect for authority, a day in which every man does that which is right in his own eyes.

No Puritan was more important for fostering a well-ordered Christian home than William Gouge (1575–1653). Among the scores of books written on marriage and family living by the Puritans, Gouge's popular *Of Domestical Duties* was the most common gift that a Puritan pastor gave to couples whose marriages he was privileged to officiate. It has recently been edited for the modern reader by Scott

---

and the Puritan Culture of Child Rearing," in *The Child in Christian Thought*, ed. Marcia J. Bunge (Grand Rapids: Eerdmans, 2001), 300–28; Ezra Hoyt Byington, *The Puritan in England and New England* (Boston: Roberts Brothers, 1897), 221–77; J. T. Cliffe, *The Puritan Gentry: The Great Puritan Families of Early Stuart England* (London: Routledge & Kegan Paul, 1984), 63–82; W. Gary Crampton, *What the Puritans Taught* (Morgan, Pa.: Soli Deo Gloria, 2003), 62–72; Gaius Davies, "The Puritan Teaching on Marriage and the Family," *The Evangelical Quarterly*, 27, no. 1 (Jan. 1955): 19–30; John Demos, *A Little Commonwealth: Family Life in Plymouth Colony* (Oxford: Oxford University Press, 1970), 82–106, 181–90; Daniel Doriani, "The Godly Household in Puritan Theology, 1560–1640" (PhD dissertation, Westminster Theological Seminary, 1985); Christopher Durston, *The Family in the English Revolution* (New York: Basil Blackwell, 1989); Alice Morse Earle, *Customs and Fashions in Old New England* (Detroit: Omnigraphics, 1990); "Form for the Confirmation of Marriage Before the Church," in *Doctrinal Standards, Liturgy, and Church Order*, ed. Joel R. Beeke (Grand Rapids: Reformation Heritage Books, 1999), 156–58; Philip J. Greven, "Family Structure in Andover," *Puritanism in Early America*, ed. George M. Waller (Lexington, Mass.: D. C. Heath and Co., 1973); William and Malleville Haller, "The Puritan Art of Love," *Huntington Library Quarterly*, 5 (1942): 235–72; Charles E. Hambrick-Stowe, "Ordering Their Private World: What the Puritans did to grow spiritually," *Christian History*, 13, no. 1 (1994): 16–19; Graham Harrison, "Marriage and Divorce in Puritan Thinking," *The Fire Divine*, Westminster Conference, 1996 (London: n.p., 1997), 27–51; Erroll Hulse, *Who Are the Puritans: And What Do They Teach?* (Darlington, England: Evangelical Press, 2000), 139–42; James Turner Johnson, *A Society Ordained by God: English Puritan Marriage Doctrine in the First Half of the Seventeenth Century* (Nashville: Abingdon, 1970); M. M. Knappen, *Tudor Puritanism: A Chapter in the History of Idealism* (Chicago: University of Chicago Press, 1965), 451–66; Morgan, *The Puritan Family*; Steven Ozment, *When Fathers Ruled: Family Life in Reformation Europe* (Cambridge, Mass.: Harvard University Press, 1983); Packer, *A Quest for Godliness*, 259–73, 355–56; Neil Pronk, "Puritan Christianity: The Puritans at Home," *The Messenger* (Sept. 1997): 3–6; Helen Ratner, "The Puritan Family," *Child & Family*, 9, no. 1 (1970): 54–60; Darrett B. Rutman, *Winthrop's Boston: A Portrait of a Puritan Town, 1630–1649* (New York: W. W. Norton Co., 1972); Leland Ryken, *Worldly Saints: The Puritans As They Really Were* (Grand Rapids: Zondervan, 1986), 39–54, 73–88; Levin Ludwig Schucking, *The Puritan Family: A Social Study from the Literary Sources* (New York: Schocken Books, 1970); Lawrence Stone, *The Family, Sex and Marriage in England 1500–1800* (New York: Harper & Row, 1977); and Margo Todd, "Humanists, Puritans and the Spiritualized Household," *Church History*, 49, no. 1 (1980): 18–34.

Brown and me and republished in three volumes under the title *Building a Godly Home.*[6]

First published in 1622, this originally seven-hundred-page penetrating analysis of the godly household is divided into eight sections dealing with the duties of family life.[7] In the first part, Gouge explains the foundation of family duties, based on Ephesians 5:21–6:9. The second part deals with the husband-wife relationship. The third focuses on the duties of wives and the fourth on the duties of husbands. The fifth examines the duties of children and the sixth the duties of parents. The final parts examine the relationships and duties of servants and their masters.[8]

While some of Gouge's material is outdated, his emphasis and advice are timeless on the whole. Brett Usher claims that Gouge is finally being "recognized as one of the subtlest of early modern writers to articulate the concept of 'companionable' marriage—his own was regarded as exemplary—and of considerate, rather than merely prescriptive, parenthood. His psychological insights into the nature of childhood and adolescence can be breathtaking in their modernity. He even touches on the question of child abuse, a subject effectively taboo until the 1970s."[9]

Gouge's valuable work unveils a skilled expositor who draws practical applications from the Epistles and personal experience in instructing families how to walk in a manner worthy of the Lord Jesus Christ. As a father of thirteen children (seven sons and six daughters), eight of whom reached maturity, Gouge knew what he was talking about. His experience as a parent was augmented the

---

6. William Gouge, *Building a Godly Home, Vol. 1, A Holy Vision for Family Life,* ed. Scott Brown and Joel R. Beeke (Grand Rapids: Reformation Heritage Books, 2013); *Building a Godly Home, Vol. 2, A Holy Vision for a Happy Marriage,* ed. Scott Brown and Joel R. Beeke (Grand Rapids: Reformation Heritage Books, 2013); *Building a Godly Home, Vol. 3, A Holy Vision for Raising Children,* ed. Scott Brown and Joel R. Beeke (Grand Rapids: Reformation Heritage Books, forthcoming 2014).

7. William Gouge, *Of Domesticall Dvties* (London: by Iohn Haviland for William Bladen, 1622).

8. The final section on masters and servants is not included in the recent three-volume modern reprint, but it is included in the 2006 edition referenced above.

9. Brett Usher, "William Gouge," in *Oxford Dictionary of National Biography,* ed. H. C. G. Matthew and Brian Harrison (Oxford: Oxford University Press, 2004), 23:38.

more when his wife died after bearing the thirteenth child, and by the fact that he never remarried.[10]

Most important, Gouge was a godly example of the matters he wrote about. His personal life was exemplary. Throughout his life, he maintained the habit of reading fifteen Bible chapters daily—five in the morning before breakfast, five after dinner, and five before going to bed. His biographer writes that his confessions of sin were accompanied with "much brokenness of heart, self-abhorrency, and justifying of God." In prayer, he was "pertinent, judicious, spiritual, seasonable, accompanied with faith and fervor, like a true Son of Jacob wrestling with tears and supplications." A contemporary wrote of Gouge: "He studied much to magnify Christ, and to debase himself." Gouge said of himself, "When I look upon myself, I see nothing but emptiness and weakness; but when I look upon Christ, I see nothing but fullness and sufficiency."[11]

Gouge's family saw in him a loving husband and father, a devout leader of family worship, a hard worker, a cheerful philanthropist, a meek friend, a great peacemaker, and an earnest wrestler with God. He had such a meek disposition that his biographer wrote, "No one, his wife, nor children, nor servant with whom he lived and worked all those years ever observed an angry countenance, nor heard an angry word proceed from him toward any of them."

Gouge suffered from asthma and kidney stones in his later years. His faith held firm, however, through acute suffering until death. He would say, "[I am] a great sinner, but I comfort myself in a great Savior." Often he repeated Job's words: "Shall we receive good at the hand of God, and shall we not receive evil?" (2:10). When a friend tried to comfort him by pointing to the grace he had received or the works he had done, his response was: "I dare not think of any such things for comfort. Jesus Christ, and what He hath done and endured, is the only ground of my sure comfort." As he approached death, he said: "Death, next to Jesus Christ, you are my best friend. When I die, I am sure to be with Jesus Christ. Jesus Christ is my rejoicing."[12]

---

10. Usher, "William Gouge," 23:37.

11. James Reid, *Memoirs of the Lives and Writings of those Eminent Divines Who Convened in the Famous Assembly at Westminster* (Paisley: Stephen and Andrew Young, 1811), 1:357.

12. Reid, *Memoirs*, 1:358.

Gouge died December 12, 1653, aged seventy-eight. In this chapter, I aim to set forth Gouge's views on Christian living, first, on marriage, and second, on raising children, drawing practical lessons from both for the Christian home today.

Gouge on a Happy Marriage

Of course, the foundation of Puritan teaching on marriage was the Word of God. Packer says, "They went to Genesis for its institution, to Ephesians for its full meaning, to Leviticus for its hygiene, to Proverbs for its management, to several New Testament books for its ethic, and to Esther, Ruth and the Song of Songs for illustrations and exhibitions of the ideal."[13] Volume 1 of *Building a Godly Home* contains Gouge's basic exposition of Ephesians 5:21–6:9. However, in subsequent material in the second volume, he gives abundant applications of Paul's teachings for wives and husbands. Let me offer you a sampling from Gouge about God's biblical purposes and biblical principles for marriage.

God's Purposes for Marriage

The medieval church's view of marriage had largely degenerated into seeing marriage as a necessity for producing children. Serious Christians were encouraged to be celibate in marriage, or better still, to become monks or nuns. On the contrary, the Puritans agreed with the Reformers that Scripture sanctifies marriage and sanctions three purposes for marriage, all of which aim for the higher good of the glory of God and the furthering of God's kingdom on earth. Gouge presented these three purposes in the same order as the Book of Common Prayer: (1) "the procreation of children, to be brought up in the fear and nurture of the Lord, and praise of God," (2) "a remedy against sin and to avoid fornication," and (3) "mutual society, help, and comfort."[14]

---

13. Packer, *A Quest for Godliness*, 263.

14. "The Form of Solemnization of Matrimony" (1549), in *The Book of Common Prayer*, ed. Brian Cummings (Oxford: Oxford University Press, 2011), 64, spelling modernized. These words and this order remained unchanged in the 1559 and 1662 editions (pp. 157, 435). Some early Puritan works on marriage maintained this order, but the Puritans gradually moved the third purpose to first place, as was codified in the 1640s by the Westminster divines in the Confession of Faith (24.2). Later Puritans focused more on the Genesis 2:18 mandate for marriage ("It is not good that the

Rooted in the creation mandate of Genesis 1:28, the first purpose for marriage, Gouge wrote, is "that the world might be increased, and not simply increased, but with a legitimate brood, and distinct families, which are the [nurseries] of cities and commonwealths, also that the church might be preserved and propagated in the world by a holy seed (Mal. 2:15)."[15] How little this is grasped in our day! Can you imagine yourself saying to your spouse, "Honey, let's try to have another child for the sake of the church, our city, and our nation"?

The second purpose for marriage is "that men might avoid fornication and possess their vessels in holiness and honor (1 Cor. 7:2). Regarding that process which is in man's corrupt nature to lust, this end adds much to the honor of marriage. It shows that marriage is a haven to those who are in jeopardy of their salvation through the gusts of temptations to lust."[16] How contemporary Gouge sounds!

The third purpose for marriage, Gouge said, is "that man and wife might be a mutual help one to another (Gen. 2:18), a help as for bringing forth, so for bringing up children, and as for erecting, so for well governing their family. A help also for well ordering prosperity, and well bearing adversity. A help in health and sickness.... In this respect it is said 'who so findeth a wife, findeth a good thing' (Prov. 18:22)."[17]

All three of these purposes are God's gift to all mankind, including unbelievers. However, in their emphasis on the earthly purposes of marriage, the Puritans did not devalue its overarching spiritual purpose. Just as Paul set forth to the Ephesians, Gouge taught that marriage is a living depiction of Christ's relationship with the church, His body (Eph. 5:22–33). The husband is to love his wife as

---

man should be alone; I will make him an help meet for him") than on the Genesis 1:28 command to be fruitful and multiply. The Dutch Reformed liturgy of the late sixteenth century had already adopted the same order, though more descriptively: "The first reason is that each faithfully assist the other in all things that belong to this life and a better. Secondly, that they bring up the children which the Lord shall give them, in the true knowledge and fear of God, to His glory, and their salvation. Third, that each of them avoiding all uncleanness and evil lusts, may live with a good and quiet conscience" (*Doctrinal Standards, Liturgy, and Church Order*, 156). Cf. Ryken, *Worldly Saints*, 48.

15. Gouge, *Building a Godly Home*, 2:29.
16. Gouge, *Building a Godly Home*, 2:29.
17. Gouge, *Building a Godly Home*, 2:30.

Christ loves the church, while the wife is to show reverence and sub-mission to her husband as the church does to Christ.

The husband's headship over his wife parallels Christ's head-ship over His church (Eph. 5:23). As Christ loves His church, the husband must exercise a "true, free, pure, exceeding, constant love" to his wife, nourishing and cherishing her as Christ does His gath-ered people.[18] Since Christ's love for His church is all-encompassing, a husband cannot love his wife adequately because, being a sinner, he always falls short of Christ's perfect love (v. 25). But Christ's love to His bride must be the husband's pattern and goal.[19] The husband must strive to love his wife absolutely (v. 25), purposely (v. 26), real-istically (v. 27), and sacrificially (vv. 28–29). Mingled together, the husband's love and the wife's respect make for a savory marriage delightful to both. Gouge wrote: "*Love* is as sugar to sweeten the duties of authority which pertain to a husband. *Respect* is as salt to season all the duties of subjection which pertain to a wife."[20]

Given the modern caricatures of Puritanism, it is vital to note that Puritan husbands were rarely male chauvinists and tyrants. Mod-elling the husband's headship on Christ's headship of the church, the Puritans understood that male authority was more a charge to responsibility than a ticket to privilege. Headship was leadership based on love (1 Peter 3:7). While the man had authority over the woman, Gouge said, "Though the man be as the head, yet is the woman as the heart."[21]

Since the church humbly and unconditionally submits to Christ, the husband's headship over his wife means that she should show reverence and yield voluntary submission to him in all things, except when her husband acts contrary to God and His commandments. For Gouge and the Puritans in general, submission was not so much a matter of hierarchy as of function. God assigns the role and duty of leadership to the husband not so he might lord over his wife, but simply to delegate authority to him and not to her. The husband is

---

18. Gouge, *Building a Godly Home*, 1:51.
19. Gouge, *Building a Godly Home*, 1:51–52.
20. Gouge, *Building a Godly Home*, 1:155–56, emphasis original.
21. Gouge, *Building a Godly Home*, 2:102.

the head, but Gouge said that God appointed the wife to be "a joint governor" with her husband over their household.[22]

Under the grand, creation-based, Christ-centered vision for the purposes of marriage, the Puritans explained the ethical principles that direct us for a God-honoring marriage.

God's Principles for Marriage

The Puritans often spoke of "duties," and Gouge was no exception. By "duty" he did not mean something done out of mere obligation and without heartfelt joy. We must serve the Lord with gladness (Ps. 100:2). But the word *duty* does remind us that God's will is not just a principle for successful living or personal fulfilment; it is God's command and our responsibility. Like most Puritans, Gouge treated the duties of marriage in three sections: mutual duties, the husband's duties, and the wife's duties. The following four principles come from Gouge's first section on mutual duties.

1. *Guard the oneness of your marriage.* The Author of marriage is God, and by His ordinance He makes two people into "one flesh" (Gen. 2:24). Gouge called this "matrimonial unity," and said that "they two who are thereby made one, [are] constantly to remain one, and not to make themselves two again." He quoted 1 Corinthians 7:10–11: "And unto the married I command, yet not I, but the Lord, Let not the wife depart from her husband: but and if she depart, let her remain unmarried or be reconciled to her husband: and let not the husband put away his wife."[23]

Husbands and wives should stay together, not only in the legal bond in marriage, but actually sharing life as they dwell together (1 Peter 3:7). At times, "weighty and urgent affairs" of church or state require absences, or one's occupation takes one away on travels for a time. But such separations should be received with sadness, and the couple should quickly return to share the same home and the same bed. The first step to helping each other is being with each other.[24]

22. Gouge, *Building a Godly Home*, 2:82–84.
23. Gouge, *Building a Godly Home*, 2:35.
24. Gouge, *Building a Godly Home*, 2:56–57.

2. *Enjoy the sexual purity of your marriage.* Gouge called this "matrimonial chastity," for the Puritans regarded as chastity not only single people abstaining from sex, but also married people enjoying sexual intimacy with their spouses (1 Cor. 7:2–4; Heb. 13:4).[25] Adultery was a horrendous crime against the marital covenant, and Gouge condemned it in both men and women.[26] To avoid this, Gouge urged spouses to give each other "due benevolence," which was a euphemism for sexual love. He wrote:

> One of the best remedies that can be prescribed to married persons (next to an awful fear of God, and a continual setting of Him before them, wherever they are) is, that husband and wife mutually delight each in the other, and maintain a pure and fervent love between themselves, yielding that due benevolence to one another which is warranted and sanctified by God's word, and ordained of God for this particular end. This "due benevolence" (as the apostle calls it [1 Cor. 7:3]) is one of the most proper and essential acts of marriage: and necessary for the main and principal ends of it.[27]

This teaching was revolutionary in its day. Marriage and especially sex had fallen under a dark cloud in the early church. Such notables as Tertullian, Ambrose, and Jerome believed that, even within marriage, intercourse necessarily involved sin.[28] This attitude inevitably led to the glorification of virginity and celibacy. By the fifth century, clerics were prohibited from marrying.[29] The archbishop of Canterbury wrote in the seventh century that a husband should never see his wife naked and that sex was forbidden on Sundays, for three days before taking Communion, and for forty days before Easter.[30] Tragically, romance became linked to mistresses and adultery, not marriage.[31]

---

25. Gouge, *Building a Godly Home*, 2:37.
26. Gouge, *Building a Godly Home*, 2:39–40.
27. Gouge, *Building a Godly Home*, 2:44.
28. Packer, *A Quest for Godliness*, 261.
29. Ryken, *Worldly Saints*, 40.
30. Theodore of Tarsus (602–690), cited in Gordon Mursell, *English Spirituality From Earliest Times to 1700* (Louisville: Westminster John Knox, 2001), 43.
31. William Haller, *The Rise of Puritanism* (New York: Harper, 1957), 122.

Puritan preachers taught that the Roman Catholic view was unbiblical, even satanic. They cited Paul, who said that the prohibition of marriage is a doctrine of devils (1 Tim. 4:1–3).[32]

The Puritans viewed sexual intimacy within marriage as a gift of God and as an essential, enjoyable part of marriage. Gouge said that husbands and wives should make love "with good will and delight, willingly, readily, and cheerfully."[33] However, the couple's sexual life should be tempered in measure and timing by proper concern for each other's piety, weakness, or illness.[34]

The ideal of marriage as romantic companionship was a far greater revolutionary concept in Puritan teaching than is often realized today. Herbert W. Richardson writes that "the rise of romantic marriage and its validation by the Puritans represents a major innovation within the Christian tradition."[35] And C. S. Lewis says that we largely owe to the Puritans "the conversion of courtly love into romantic monogamous love."[36]

3. *Love your spouse and live in harmony.* This is commanded of husbands in Ephesians 5:25 and of wives in Titus 2:4. Gouge wrote: "A loving mutual affection must pass between husband and wife, or else no duty will be well performed. This is the ground of all the rest."[37] Each should cherish the other as a special gift from God's mercy.[38] Each should seek to maintain peace with the other so that they may live together in harmony (Heb. 12:14). To your spouse you should be like a haven in a storm-tossed world: "If the haven be calm, and free from storms and tempests, what a refreshing it will be to the mariner that has been tossed in the sea with winds and waves?"[39] But he warned, "Discord between man and wife in

---

32. Ryken, *Worldly Saints*, 42.

33. Gouge, *Building a Godly Home*, 2:44.

34. Gouge, *Building a Godly Home*, 2:46.

35. Herbert W. Richardson, *Nun, Witch, Playmate: The Americanization of Sex* (New York: Harper & Row, 1971), 69.

36. C. S. Lewis, "Donne and Love Poetry in the Seventeenth Century," in *Seventeenth Century Studies Presented to Sir Herbert Grierson* (Oxford: Oxford University Press, 1938), 75.

37. Gouge, *Building a Godly Home*, 2:47.

38. Gouge, *Building a Godly Home*, 2:48–50.

39. Gouge, *Building a Godly Home*, 2:52.

a house is as contention between the master and pilot in a ship"—
extremely dangerous to both.[40]

Gouge said that your spouse is your "companion."[41] He wrote:
"Neither friend, nor child, nor parent ought so to be loved as a wife.
She is termed, 'the wife of his bosom' (Deut. 13:6), to show that she
ought to be as his heart in his bosom.... [She is] nearer than sister,
mother, daughter, friend, or any other whoever."[42]

4. *Build up each other's souls with prayer.* Spouses must seek the good
of each other's souls.[43] Gouge wrote, "Prayer is a mutual duty which
one owes to the other, which Isaac performed for his wife" (Gen.
25:21). He counselled married couples to pray together in private, lifting up requests to God that they would be "one spirit" just as they
are one flesh, "that their hearts may be as one, knit together by a true,
spiritual, matrimonial love, always delighting one in another, ever
helpful to one another, and ready with all willingness and cheerful-
ness to perform all those duties which they owe to one another."
They should pray for God to sanctify their sexual life, give them children, save their children, provide their family's financial needs, and
fill them with all the gifts and spiritual graces they need.[44]

Gouge went on to give instructions about spouses helping each
other to overcome temptation and grow spiritually. They must pray
for one another, compliment one another, appreciate one another,
and "keep the unity of the spirit in the bond of peace" with one
another. They must not speak harshly to or provoke each other, but
must show kindness to each other and overlook each other's minor
faults. They must cultivate true friendship and take an interest in
each other. They must be sympathetic to each other in times of
distress, sickness, and weakness. They must promote each other's
reputation, never speaking ill of each other in the presence of others.
They must be confidential, not revealing each other's secrets. Finally,
Gouge exhorted them to care for each other's physical needs, to manage their possessions well, to share their oversight of the household,

---

40. Gouge, *Building a Godly Home*, 2:54.
41. Gouge, *Building a Godly Home*, 2:188.
42. Gouge, *Building a Godly Home*, 2:181.
43. Gouge, *Building a Godly Home*, 2:61.
44. Gouge, *Building a Godly Home*, 2:62.

and to work together to serve others in hospitality and benevolence to the poor.[45]

In the areas of the specific duties of husbands and wives, too, Gouge presents us with a number of striking thoughts. I shall be very brief in summarizing them.

Husbands should delight in their wives (Prov. 5:18–19), esteeming them, respecting them, and seeking to please them, even to the point that others consider it "doting." Husbands should not allow blemishes in their wives to slacken their affection for them, either. Gouge said, "If a man have a wife, not very beautiful or proper, but having some deformity in her body, some imperfection in speech, sight, gesture, or any part of her body," he ought yet be so affectionate to her, "and delight in her, as if she were the most beautiful and in every way the most perfect woman in the world."[46]

Then, too, a husband must provide for his wife in sickness and in health. He must particularly assist her when she is pregnant.[47] He must bestow favors, kindnesses, and gifts on her. He must never strike her or abuse her verbally or physically. At times, a husband might reprove his wife, but only in tender love and always to steer her away from sin. Reproofs, however, should be rare and administered in private with humility—never when his wife is angry.[48] Finally, a husband must accept the functions that his wife performs. He must show his acceptance by his gratitude, by not demanding too much from her, and by giving her freedom to manage the affairs of the home. He must do all this cheerfully and tenderly.[49]

In addition to showing submission and reverence to her husband and fulfilling mutual marital duties, a wife has numerous unique responsibilities. She should be content with her husband's work, social standing, and financial status. Her conversations with him should also show respect, and she should be willing to move to "dwell where her husband will have her dwell."

Then, too, she should manage the affairs of the household effectively (Proverbs 31). As a helpmeet for her husband (Gen. 2:18), she

---

45. Gouge, *Building a Godly Home*, 2:73–81.
46. Gouge, *Building a Godly Home*, 2:194.
47. Gouge, *Building a Godly Home*, 2:241–42.
48. Gouge, *Building a Godly Home*, 2:215–24.
49. Gouge, *Building a Godly Home*, 2:196–236.

should assist him in a variety of ways, showing wise leadership skills in the home, understanding clearly in what areas she should dialogue with her husband and ask for his consent and in what areas she has liberty to manage on her own. Such management includes helping her husband establish Christ's kingdom in their home as a little church; being thrifty without being miserly; consistently persevering in completing her duties; and handling herself with sobriety, mildness, courtesy, obeisance, and modesty, as the Bible commands.[50]

In summary, Gouge presented a remarkably insightful treatment of the beauty and glory of Christian marriage. His vision for matrimony was holistic and practical, yet very much centered around the Lord. Husbands and wives have different roles, but do not live on separate levels. Instead they live together as companions and coworkers for the glory of God, for the good of each other, and for the good of others, especially their children.

Gouge on the Beauty and Glory of Raising Children

The Christian's relationship with his family is inseparable from personal sanctification, according to the Puritans. The Scriptures set forth the ways in which we are to live righteously, and since the Bible takes great pains to teach how parents and children should relate to one another, these relationships are an index of sanctification. So it is of primary importance that Christians recognize that holiness and the beauty of Christian living begin at home and then extend to all of life.

While most Puritans believed that the primary purpose of marriage was companionship, they also believed that having children was an expected consequence of marital love. Children were seen as blessings of the Lord. And apparently they were blessings that the Lord bestowed frequently and abundantly. Puritan families were large, with an average of seven or eight children. The infant mortality rate was also very high, however. Typically, of all the children born in a family, only half reached adulthood.

The Puritans were keenly aware that children were a tremendous responsibility, viewing their families as nurseries for church and society. Parents were expected to do everything possible to make sure their children conformed to biblical norms and precepts, especially the commandment to obey their parents.

---

50. Gouge, *Building a Godly Home*, 2:98–179.

The taproot of Puritan teaching on parents and children was the fifth commandment (Ex. 20:12), which Paul quotes in his instructions to households in Ephesians 6:1–4: "Children, obey your parents in the Lord: for this is right. Honour thy father and mother; which is the first commandment with promise; that it may be well with thee, and thou mayest live long on the earth. And, ye fathers, provoke not your children to wrath: but bring them up in the nurture and admonition of the Lord."

In Gouge's application of Paul's words to the Ephesians, he devoted well over a hundred pages in volume 3 to the relationships between children and parents. Let me give you a taste of his teaching by addressing the spirit of parenting and the tasks of parenting.

The Spirit of Parenting: Authority and Love

Gouge traced out the essence of parenting in terms of authority and love. He taught that parents must raise their children with a mixture of "authority and affection," which moves children to respond with childlike "fear" and "love." He compared it to cooking with both sugar and salt: both are needed for a tasty meal lest it be too sweet or bitter.[51] A child's love is a response to his parent's affection for him; like the sun shining on a stone, "so the hot beams of parents' love" shining constantly should warm their children to reflect love back.[52] By fear, he did not mean dread or terror that drives a child away, but a high esteem with a sincere desire to please the parents and hatred of offending them.[53]

God calls both the father and the mother to this noble task, and invests both parents with proper authority to exercise it. The father has first place in the family, both in "dignity" and "duty," because he is the head of the household (Eph. 5:23).[54] But that does not make the wife into a servant in the home. Gouge noted that the fifth commandment requires honoring both "father and mother," and taught that children owe "equal respect" to both parents.[55] He wrote, "Though there is a difference between father and mother in relation of one to

---

51. Gouge, *Building a Godly Home*, vol. 3, ch. 1.
52. Gouge, *Building a Godly Home*, vol. 3, ch. 1.
53. Gouge, *Building a Godly Home*, vol. 3, ch. 1.
54. Gouge, *Building a Godly Home*, 1:33.
55. Gouge, *Building a Godly Home*, vol. 3, ch. 5.

another, in relation to their children they are both as one, and have a like authority over them."[56]

This reverent respect should lead children to restrain their own talking around their parents (Job 29:9–10) and to listen patiently when their parents speak (Job 29:21). They must not be insolent, complain, or slink away before their parents have finished speaking.[57] Gouge noted that the Greek word for "obey" in Ephesians 6:1 means "to listen with humble submission."[58] When children speak to their parents, they should use respectful titles such as "Father" and "Mother"; speak humbly, briefly, and with their parents' permission; not interrupt their parents' work or conversations; and give a ready answer when their parents ask a question.[59] Honoring their father and their mother also means speaking respectfully about them when they are not present and not slandering them.[60]

The Puritans understood that Christian obedience must come from the heart, but they also understood that the "disposition of the heart" shows itself in "action." So Gouge expected children to honor their parents in posture, gestures, and facial expressions.[61] They must not be rude to their father and mother.[62] Of course, Ephesians 6:1 requires children to obey their parents, and Gouge spent more than twenty pages discussing how they should not do what their parents have not given them permission to do, and how they should listen to what their parents command.[63]

All their obedience is governed by the phrase "in the Lord" (Eph. 6:1), which "puts forth a limitation, direction, and motivation": limiting children's obedience by the laws of Christ, directing them to obey their parents with "an eye to Christ," and motivating them by the fact that their parents exercise authority as those who "bear the image of Christ."[64]

---

56. Gouge, *Building a Godly Home*, vol. 3, ch. 5.
57. Gouge, *Building a Godly Home*, vol. 3, ch. 1.
58. Gouge, *Building a Godly Home*, 1:161.
59. Gouge, *Building a Godly Home*, vol. 3, ch. 1.
60. Gouge, *Building a Godly Home*, vol. 3, ch. 1.
61. Gouge, *Building a Godly Home*, vol. 3, ch. 1.
62. Gouge, *Building a Godly Home*, vol. 3, ch. 1.
63. Gouge, *Building a Godly Home*, vol. 3, chs. 1–3.
64. Gouge, *Building a Godly Home*, 1:162.

Parents do not merely rule; they serve God. Fathers and mothers must likewise remember that they "are as well bound to duty as children." Gouge explained, "Though parents are over their children and cannot be commanded by them, they are under God."[65] Someone might object that the fifth commandment addresses only children and lays no duties on parents when it says, "Honour thy father and thy mother." Gouge replied that the law implies obligation on the parents by "good and necessary consequence," for "they who have honor must carry themselves worthy of honor."[66]

Though parental authority is the skeleton and backbone that structures the raising of children, the living flesh and blood of parenting is love. Gouge said that the "fountain" or source of all that parents should do must be "love." Titus 2:4 urges that young women be trained "to love their children." The Lord said to Abraham, "Take now thy son, thine only son Isaac, *whom thou lovest*" (Gen. 22:2, emphasis added). The work of a father and mother costs them much labor, money, and care, but if they love their children, nothing seems too much. God has planted love for children in parents by nature, and Christians should fan this fire into flame.[67] Out of the fountain of parental love flow many streams, and this brings us to consider the tasks of parenting.

The Tasks of Parenting: Provident Care of Body and Soul
Paul commands fathers to "bring up" their children (Eph. 6:4), which Gouge pointed out means "to feed or nourish with everything needed." Yet the apostle immediately qualifies this with the words "in the nurture and admonition of the Lord," showing "that nurture and instruction are as necessary and profitable as food and clothing."[68] Gouge placed the entire spectrum of a father's and mother's duties under the heading of "provident care for their children's good."[69] By "provident care," he meant that parents not only meet the immediate needs of their children, but also look ahead and prepare them for their future both on earth and in eternity.[70]

---

65. Gouge, *Building a Godly Home*, 1:185.
66. Gouge, *Building a Godly Home*, 1:185–86.
67. Gouge, *Building a Godly Home*, vol. 3, ch. 6.
68. Gouge, *Building a Godly Home*, 1:189–90.
69. Gouge, *Building a Godly Home*, vol. 3, ch. 6.
70. Gouge, *Building a Godly Home*, 1:180.

Out of the wealth of teaching Gouge offered, let me cull twelve tasks for parents.

1. *Pray for your children.* Gouge said that prayer "is the first and it is the last duty which parents ought to perform to their children."[71] There is nothing parents can do for their children that does them more good than prayer. They should pray before their children are born (Gen. 25:21; 1 Sam. 1:10) and all their lives (Job. 1:5), for children are conceived in sin, but the Lord is a covenant-keeping God who loves to bless the children of believers.[72]

2. *Walk in godliness for God's blessing on your children.* Gouge noted that part of God's reward to righteous people is a blessing on their children. Psalm 112:2 says, "His seed shall be mighty upon earth: the generation of the upright shall be blessed." We cannot save our children by our faith, but many blessings, earthly and spiritual, come to the offspring of the righteous.[73]

3. *Care for your children in the womb.* Gouge urged the pregnant woman to "have a special care" for her child as soon as she knows that she is pregnant. Fathers "must be tender over their wives, and helpful to them in all things needful" when they are with child. He warned that those who intentionally kill a child in the womb are "guilty of blood, even of willful murder," for that child has a "soul formed in it by God."[74]

4. *Nurture your children in infancy.* Here Gouge admitted, "What the particulars are women better know than I can express."[75] Interestingly, he made an extended argument that mothers should breastfeed their own children rather than give them to others to nurse.[76]

---

71. Gouge, *Building a Godly Home*, vol. 3, ch. 6.
72. Gouge, *Building a Godly Home*, vol. 3, ch. 6.
73. Gouge, *Building a Godly Home*, vol. 3, ch. 6.
74. Gouge, *Building a Godly Home*, vol. 3, ch. 6.
75. Gouge, *Building a Godly Home*, vol. 3, ch. 6.
76. Gouge, *Building a Godly Home*, vol. 3, ch. 6.

5. *Have your children baptized.* Gouge did not believe that baptism had any inherent power to save sinners.[77] But he believed that God's command that the men of Abraham's household should circumcise their sons implied that Christians should have their children baptized (Gen. 17:10). Parents should see that their child is rightly baptized by a minister of the Word (Matt. 28:19).[78] In baptism, Christian parents assume covenant responsibilities on behalf of their children. God, therefore, claims these children as His own; parents are stewards of their children on God's behalf.

6. *Provide your children with necessities for health.* He specifically mentioned food, clothing, medical care, and recreation—the last of which is notable because some people think the Puritans were against all kinds of fun. On the contrary, Gouge noted that the prophet Zechariah rejoices over a vision of "boys and girls playing" (8:5).[79] However, Gouge also noted Proverbs 27:7, "The full soul loatheth an honeycomb," and warned that too much food, fancy clothing, pampering, or play time weakens both body and mind, and traps children in immaturity.[80]

7. *Give your children a good moral education.* He wrote, "Learning would much sharpen their wits.... Good education is better than a great portion."[81] By education, he meant training a child how to order the whole course of his life. Part of this is training in "good manners," the outward beauty of a well-ordered life. Gouge had no illusions that good manners could save a person or substitute for inward grace. But he also believed that rudeness and a lack of courtesy and kindness were not consistent with grace.[82]

8. *Give your children a good vocational education.* Another part of education for Gouge was preparing a child for "a good calling," that is, a vocation or honest means to support himself and his family, help

---

77. Gouge, *Building a Godly Home*, 1:69–79.
78. Gouge, *Building a Godly Home*, vol. 3, ch. 6.
79. Gouge, *Building a Godly Home*, vol. 3, ch. 6.
80. Gouge, *Building a Godly Home*, vol. 3, ch. 6.
81. Gouge, *Building a Godly Home*, vol. 3, ch. 6.
82. Gouge, *Building a Godly Home*, vol. 3, ch. 7.

the poor, serve his society, and avoid a wasted life.[83] This requires education in fundamentals such as reading and writing, and preparation for a kind of work approved by the general principles of God's Word. Here parents must find the calling for which their child is best equipped in body and mind—not just to make a lot of money, but to glorify God.[84]

9. *Train your children in godliness.* Gouge said that Ephesians 6:4 mandates training in "true piety" with the words "in the...admonition of the Lord." He wrote, "Learning, civility, calling, portion, are all nothing without piety."[85] Fathers have a special responsibility to maintain family devotions so that the family prays, sings psalms, and reads the Word together. They are to teach the Bible with "forceful and frequent" applications "to fix and settle them in the mind of their children."[86] Children are not born Christians, but with hearts already totally inclined to evil (Gen. 6:5; Job 11:12). Parents should not say, "That is the minister's job," because God explicitly commands them in Deuteronomy 6:7, "thou shalt teach them diligently unto thy children." The parent is "a king, a priest, and a prophet" for children in the home, and who knows children better than their own parents?[87] Teach them with daily catechism, real life, and your example.[88]

10. *Discipline your children with rebuke and the rod.* This, Gouge pointed out, is what the word *nurture* in Ephesians 6:4 means: correction with instruction. Discipline must be neither too strict nor too slack, for, he said, "slackness will make children careless of all duty to God and parent; rigor will make them despair."[89] If verbal reproof is ineffective, the rod must be used as "a means appointed by God," Gouge said, "to help good nurture and education of children. It is the last remedy that a parent can use: a remedy which may do good when

---

83. Gouge, *Building a Godly Home*, vol. 3, ch. 7.
84. Gouge, *Building a Godly Home*, vol. 3, ch. 7.
85. Gouge, *Building a Godly Home*, vol. 3, ch. 7.
86. Gouge, *Building a Godly Home*, 1:191.
87. Gouge, *Building a Godly Home*, vol. 3, ch. 7. For practical tips on parenting under the offices of Christ, see Joel R. Beeke, *Parenting by God's Promises: How to Raise Children in the Covenant of Grace* (Orlando, Fla.: Reformation Trust, 2011), chaps. 6–14.
88. Gouge, *Building a Godly Home*, vol. 3, ch. 7.
89. Gouge, *Building a Godly Home*, 1:190–91.

nothing else can."[90] Spanking of young children must be measured according to the offense committed, however, and must be done in a timely manner, with love, compassion, prayer, and self-control.[91] Love in no way contradicts the parents' calling to exercise authority over their children. The opposite is true: parents do good to their children by training them to obey, for God promises to bless obedient children (Eph. 6:3).[92]

11. *Provide your children with the means to get started in their vocations and families.* Parents should save up for their children (2 Cor. 12:14) so that when they become young adults, they can give them help to launch out into life (Gen. 25:5–6).[93]

12. *Help your children find good spouses.* Though our present culture would make marriage a matter primarily of individual romance, Gouge reminded us that in Scripture parents bear a responsibility for the marriages of their children (Gen. 24:4; Jer. 29:6). They must help them find spouses well suited for them (Gen. 2:18). He did not believe that children should marry without their parents' blessing, but also did not think parents should force a child to marry someone. Marriage requires "a mutual liking" so that "the parties may willingly with mutual consent join themselves together."[94]

Christian parents were to help their young people select a suitable mate for life by considering five major criteria: (1) Would the proposed spouse walk with their son or daughter with wisdom and genuine godliness in marriage? Such qualities were necessary for the marriage to be "in the Lord." (2) Would the proposed spouse fit the biblical description of what a marriage partner is to be? Did the proposed husband have good leadership skills and a loving demeanor? Did the proposed wife show submission and reverence to her own father? A biblical mind-set about marriage and a character that reflected that mind-set was of utmost importance. (3) Was the proposed spouse mature and properly motivated for entering into marriage? It was

---

90. Gouge, *Building a Godly Home*, vol. 3, ch. 8.
91. Gouge, *Building a Godly Home*, vol. 3, ch. 8.
92. Gouge, *Building a Godly Home*, 1:180.
93. Gouge, *Building a Godly Home*, vol. 3, ch. 9.
94. Gouge, *Building a Godly Home*, vol. 3, ch. 9.

necessary to avoid marrying out of wrong motivations, such as the love of money or power. (4) Was the proposed spouse fairly equal to their son or daughter in terms of class and financial resources? It was necessary to avoid being "unequally yoked" culturally and socially, because people did not change classes often or easily three centuries ago. (5) Was the proposed spouse somewhat attractive in the eyes of their son or daughter? It was felt that there should be at least some romantic spark to begin with, though the Puritans taught that most romance would develop after marriage. Note that appearance was the last and least matter to be concerned about; marriages were to be built more on character than on appearance.

Conclusion

Though the Puritans did not worship the family, they recognized the central place of the family in God's plans for His glory and for the beauty and glory of Christian living. Gouge said, "A family is a little church and a little nation"; in the family are trained the Christians, citizens, officers, and officials of the future.[95] Though we should not follow them slavishly, the Puritans can help us regain the biblical vision for a godly home. In a demonized culture, they help us to see the essential goodness of all that God has created (1 Tim. 4:1–4). In a secularized culture, their words call us to sanctify our marriages and family life by filling them with thanksgiving, the Word of God, and prayer (1 Tim. 4:4–5). In a hyper-sexualized culture, they help us to rebuild the structures of marital sexuality and gender differences so that men and women can flourish in masculinity and femininity. In an anti-authoritarian culture, the Puritans show how authority enables love and honors God.

In many ways, the biblical vision for marriage and raising children comes to us as law. It reveals our sins, uncovers the rebellion of our hearts, humbles us for our wickedness, and displays the justice of God, who rightly condemns those who reject His beautiful, righteous ways.

However, the Bible's call to build a godly home also comes to us as gospel—good news. The best of husbands is but a shadow of Jesus Christ, who loved His people in their uncleanness and gave Himself to wash away their guilt and to purify their lives. The most

---

95. Gouge, *Building a Godly Home*, 1:20.

submissive of wives is but an instance of the great beauty of the true church, which humbly trusts and obeys Jesus as her Lord and Savior. The wisest of parents is a tiny image of the Father in heaven, who adopts sinners into His family and trains them with Word and suffering for eternal life in glory.

You see, the biblical family is ultimately about God's grace for sinners. It calls us to trust in a gracious Savior and to turn from all that has controlled us to follow Him. You cannot build a godly family merely by scriptural teaching plus human willpower. You can walk in this path only by grace alone, in Christ alone, through faith alone, and for the glory of God alone. As Gouge said so beautifully, "Sanctification is not a cause, but an effect of Christ's love, and follows after His love."[96] May the love of Christ penetrate your soul, fill your whole being, and transform all your relationships—including those in your own home—so that the beauty and glory of Christian living may shine in your marriage and your family to God's superlative glory.

---

96. Gouge, *Building a Godly Home*, 1:63.

CHAPTER 6

Living in the Workplace: Following in Jesus' Steps

William VanDoodewaard

Servants, be subject to your masters with all fear; not only to the good and gentle, but also to the froward. For this is thankworthy, if a man for conscience toward God endure grief, suffering wrongfully. For what glory is it, if, when ye be buffeted for your faults, ye shall take it patiently? but if, when ye do well, and suffer for it, ye take it patiently, this is acceptable with God. For even hereunto were ye called: because Christ also suffered for us, leaving us an example, that ye should follow his steps: who did no sin, neither was guile found in his mouth: who, when he was reviled, reviled not again; when he suffered, he threatened not; but committed himself to him that judgeth righteously: who his own self bare our sins in his own body on the tree, that we, being dead to sins, should live unto righteousness: by whose stripes ye were healed. For ye were as sheep going astray; but are now returned unto the Shepherd and Bishop of your souls.

—1 Peter 2:18–25

Many of us give little thought to the way we speak about or even to our bosses, managers, or employers. Nearly all of us have experienced a time in life when it was hard to maintain respect for someone in authority over us in the workplace. Our culture views complaint and disrespect as inalienable rights, normalizing them in everything from comic strips such as *Dilbert* to evening sitcoms such as *The Office*. Our entertainment media both reflect and accelerate our work culture tendencies—the sin of fallen hearts and the misery that they produce.

But what does God desire for our work relationships? What is His design for us and the work cultures we help create?

Submitting with All Respect

In 1 Peter 2:18–25, God's Word addresses the way we relate to people under whose authority we work. Penned by the apostle Peter under the inspiration of the Holy Spirit, the first words of this passage read, "Servants, be subject to your masters."

In the early New Testament context, slavery was a widespread fact of life. There were those who were slaves due to military conquest, while others were slaves because of outstanding debts or poverty. Some would serve out their lives to pay off debts (and in some cases, when the debt was very great, their children would also serve their entire lives). In the Roman Empire, slaves performed a wide variety of tasks in society. Many farm and construction workers were slaves; some were managers of estates, teachers, and physicians. In many ways, it was a radically different world from ours.

Yet while we have greater freedom in employment, mobility, and life decisions, we are also under authority in our work. Like the slaves and servants of Peter's day, we also have "masters"—and God's enduring Word calls us to submit to them. In fact, part of Peter's concern, revealed in previous verses (cf. v. 16), is to guard us against using our Christian liberty to claim that we are exempt from the authority and order of master-servant relationships. This is as much a radical concept today as it was then: the triune God, the Creator of all things, the Redeemer, calls us, as Christians, to submit to those in authority over us in the workplace.

What does it mean to submit? Commentator Alexander Nisbet speaks of Christians' calling to carry out the "common duties...owed to their masters."[1] He states that submitting "consists...in obeying all their lawful commands heartily."[2] John Calvin sees the call to "be subject" or to submit as the call "for the obedience of servants to masters."[3] John Brown more extensively comments:

> Let your will be regulated by their will...be submissive to their arrangements. Servants are to be obedient to the commands of

---

1. Alexander Nisbet, *An Exposition of 1 & 2 Peter* (Edinburgh: Banner of Truth, 1982), 100. Quotes from commentaries by Alexander Nisbet, John Calvin, John Brown, and Robert Leighton are rendered in contemporary English in this chapter.
2. Nisbet, *Exposition*, 100.
3. John Calvin, *Commentaries on The Catholic Epistles*, trans. John Owen (Grand Rapids: Baker, 1981), 86.

their master; that is, they are to do what their master bids them, in the way in which he requires it to be done, to the best of their ability.… A servant has taken a price for his time and his capacity of labour, and it is but just that he who has bought them should dispose of them. They are no more his than his wages are his master's. He is a person under authority.[4]

In verse 18, we are told what the character of our submitting is to be. It is not merely a "technical" submission, like the slave following the master's orders, but doing so with bitterness and hatred toward the man, or like the construction worker who carries out his duties while full of disdain for his foreman. Neither are we to submit simply "because we have to" in order to maintain an income or job stability. Submission, while foundational, is not enough; neither is it enough to add occasional respect as we submit to workplace authority.

Rather, a real, full respect is essential to God-honoring submission. Through Peter, our Lord calls us to submit to our masters *with all respect*. This *all respect* is not a false front or a fleeting mood, but genuine and steady. It is a respect that is sincere and abiding. It is inseparably connected to the fear of God; a spirit of profound reverence and respect toward God is the source for workplace respect. The kingdom of God, expressed by His Word and the lives of His people, is marked by a beautiful, honorable integrity in respectful submission toward those in workplace authority.

But what if the directives of your "master" are immoral or evil? What if they are foolish or unwise? Of course, the call to submit with all respect to our earthly masters does not mean a submission that follows orders to violate the law of God. As Peter said to the Sanhedrin, if earthly authorities contravene God's Word and try to bind others to the same, we must then obey God rather than men (Acts 4:19–20; 5:29). Neither does all respect mean having to do the impossible. Brown states:

A master has, can have, no right to command what is impracticable, what is not in the servant's power; and therefore in such cases the servant is under no obligation to obedience. The Israelites were not to blame when they did not obey Pharaoh, commanding them to make bricks, when he withheld from

---

4. John Brown, *Expository Discourses on the First Epistle of the Apostle Peter* (Marshallton, Del.: The National Foundation for Christian Education, n.d.), 144.

them straw. There is nothing wrong in a servant refusing to attempt what he knows to be an impossibility, or what he is aware cannot be done, or attempted to be done, without materially injuring him.[5]

The call to submit with all respect also does not mean that we are barred from voicing concerns in matters of wisdom or thoughts that might be helpful, but it does mean that when we "submit" our opinions, concerns, and wisdom, we do that very thing—we submit them for consideration, leaving the decision respectfully to whom it belongs. Where we have seen wrongs, injustices, or error that must be countered, submission means pursuing the right in a manner that retains respect for the order and positions that God has providentially ordained. Finally, the call for servants to submit to their masters in no way justifies any sin on the part of "masters": God has given abundant counsel in His Word for those who find themselves in workplace authority over others. They stand accountable before God, men, and angels for the way they exercise their authority (cf. Eph. 6:9).

The end of verse 18 heightens our calling as Christian "servants," leaving us without excuse as to the breadth of the *all respect* to which we are called. We are to live it "not only to the good and gentle, but also to the froward"—to those who are unreasonable. "To the good and to the unreasonable" covers all the possibilities. It includes the employer who is wise and good, a delight to work for. It also includes the okay, the tolerable, the mediocre, and the unreasonable employer. Even the good Christian employer may display occasional mediocrity, perhaps even unreasonableness, due to remaining sin. To each of these types of people, when we are in their employment under their authority, we are to submit to their leadership and authority *with all respect!*

This is powerfully reinforced in verse 19. Here Peter, by the Spirit, tells us "this is thankworthy, if a man for conscience toward God endure[s] grief, suffering wrongfully." The following verse ties in closely. Asking what glory there is if we patiently receive a deserved beating for wrongdoing (the obvious answer: none!), Peter then sets a decided contrast: "but if, when ye do well, and suffer for it, ye take it patiently, this is acceptable with God." There are important truths

---

5. Brown, *Expository Discourses*, 145.

we need to note here. First, our Lord does not ignore our humanity or the reality of how frustrating, painful, and hard it is to experience injustice as a result of doing good. He knows the reality of this kind of grief, even as He gives us the high calling of pursuing fullness of respect and submission through it. Second, He also gives great encouragement in letting us know that when the believer, for the sake of "conscience toward God," endures injustice from an unreasonable master with patience, pursuing God's calling to be a respectful servant, it is "thankworthy." It is praiseworthy, a delight to God. It is also otherworldly; continued submission with *all respect* while enduring unjust suffering can truly occur only as a fruit of the Spirit.

The early church of Asia Minor undoubtedly had in its number those who were literal slaves and servants. Most had no option of changing masters, no possibility of finding new employers if they were harshly treated. Their masters often owned them as property. Slaves and servants could and did receive physical beatings and deprivations. If God's Word called them to richly manifest respect and regard for order and authority, how much more should we? What a marvelous testimony of God's grace it was for a slave who had endured injustice to then turn to his master afterward and, with a real respect, take up the next task he requested! It was a radical, otherworldly, remarkable testimony of the grace of God in the servant. Robert Leighton comments:

> This declares to us the freeness of the grace of God...that He often bestows the riches of his grace on persons of humble condition.... The honour of a spiritual royalty may be concealed under the humility of a servant.... It may happen that a perverse crooked-minded master may have an upright and honest servant, endowed with a tender conscience towards God. This the Lord does to counteract the pride of man, and to display the lustre of His own free grace. Grace...whether it find a man high or low, a master or a servant, does not require a change of his station, but works a change in his heart, and teaches him how to live in it.... Grace forms a man to a Christian way of walking in any estate.[6]

---

6. Robert Leighton, *A Practical Commentary Upon The First Epistle of St. Peter* (London: SPCK, 1849), 1:392–393

Most of us, if an employer tries to physically, financially, or even emotionally abuse us, have legitimate recourse to the law. Employers usually also have detailed contractual obligations to which they must adhere. We have the freedom of being able to resign positions and seek other employment. Yet even as God in His providence has given us just processes to deal with many situations, how much more should we walk by the same spirit, the same heart attitude of submitting in all lawful tasks, with all respect through the duration of our (often significantly lesser) workplace struggles and injustices. Why should a first-century slave or a present-day Christian employee live this way on the job? Because, as Peter emphasizes in verse 20 and the beginning of verse 21, you and I have been called to this purpose by God and it is pleasing to Him. Our chief end is to glorify God and to enjoy Him forever.[7] This in itself is a glorious and awesome reason to submit to our workday masters with all respect: God desires this of us; it is holy and good; it honors Him. But the text doesn't stop there. Peter goes on to show us that living with respectful submission to our employers is to actively live the gospel of our Lord Jesus Christ, both by following His example and looking to Him for grace.

Following the Example of Christ

As the apostle brings us the Word of God, calling us to this way of life on the job, he points us to Jesus. Christ suffered for you, he says, and He left you an example. He desires that you follow in His steps. We see in verse 21 that our Lord Jesus Christ, the only begotten Son of God, not only suffered for us to accomplish the great exchange of redemption, but He also willingly suffered to be able to leave us the perfect example of living the way God intends life to be lived. Peter calls us to look to Jesus' example, practically applied to the way that we relate to those with workplace authority over us.

Verses 22–23 remind us that Jesus committed no sin: no deceit was found in His mouth; while being reviled, He did not revile in return; when suffering, He uttered no threats; and through it all, He kept on entrusting Himself to Him who judges righteously. In doing all of this, our Lord Jesus Christ was glorifying the Father. He was magnifying the law, living out God's intention for respect, order, and peace in life. He was living out the law in perfect beauty and

---

7. Westminster Shorter Catechism, Question 1.

holiness in a sin-loving, God-hating, hostile world. You see, Jesus is the perfect, awesome, beautiful, complete embodiment of God's law. His example is exactly what you and I are called to. Leighton reflects: "Christ's spotlessness and patience in suffering are both set before us here.... Whoever you are who makes such a noise about the injustice of what you suffer, thinking you justify your impatience by your innocence, let me ask you: are you more just and innocent than He who is set before you here?"[8]

This is profoundly sobering. God has called us all to live with all respect: with respectful submission even in situations when we are suffering personal injustice. The way Jesus lived displays the fullness of respect and submission to earthly masters that we are called to have every moment of every workday, every evening after work, every weekend. God's holiness and the holy requirements of His law are brilliantly displayed here, and they expose our own darkness, our own sin. His Word provides us with a view, through Christ, of the reality of ourselves. We have fallen short, far short, of God's calling to us. We have often done the exact opposite! But with Paul and Peter, we can rejoice. Thanks be to God for inspiring these verses for us; thanks be to God for revealing His holy will, our sin, and the beauty of Christ's perfect example!

Looking to Jesus

Already in verse 21, the Spirit has graciously pointed us to Christ as the one who "suffered for us." Not only has He magnified the holiness of God and the perfection of His law through suffering, not only has He gone before us to show us the perfect pattern for the life of the sons of God, but He is also the perfect Savior for us. Leighton says, "This is the main ground of our confidence in Him, that He is a holy, harmless, undefiled High Priest."[9] Peter states in verse 24 that Jesus Christ Himself bore our sins in His body on the cross. He is the blameless and innocent Lamb who suffered, was reviled, and was slain. In His humiliation and suffering, He committed Himself to Him who judges righteously[10] (v. 23).

---

8. Leighton, *A Practical Commentary*, 407.
9. Leighton, *A Practical Commentary*, 407.
10. Leighton, *A Practical Commentary*, 410.

As Peter declares the person and work of Christ to us in verses 23 and 24, two beautiful aspects of the work of Christ are brought together. Theologians refer to these as Christ's "active" and "passive" obedience in His great work of atonement, the accomplishment of redemption. "Passive obedience" refers to Jesus' willingness to take on Himself the penalty and punishment due for our sin. Every sin deserves the wrath and curse of God. Christ's great self-sacrifice, His penal, atoning substitution in His sufferings to death, wherein His body was broken and His blood shed, completely satisfied the justice that His people deserved. "Active obedience" refers to Jesus' fulfillment of all righteousness, His perfect obedience of God's law. This includes His submission with all respect to earthly authorities, even when mistreated and abused to death. His active obedience was essential to make His suffering and death a worthy and sufficient substitutionary satisfaction for us.

Both Jesus' active and passive obedience are "charged to the account" of believers. As we receive them by faith, they are credited to us, imputed to us, just as He willingly received the imputation of our sins to Himself. The result is that the Christian is not just forgiven for all his or her sin, but also stands clothed in the righteousness of Christ. Christ's perfect holiness, His perfect goodness, covers us.

When we think of Jesus' earthly life, His suffering and death, we need to think of this total, immense package. The wonder of it is that Christ's perfect example of living with all respect, which would condemn us to eternal damnation, is instead what is credited to you and me as Christians. With Christ's atoning death, the penalty of the infinite wrath we have earned, along with the requirement of righteousness, is satisfied. Now united with Christ, we are freely declared righteous, reconciled to God, adopted as His children, and enabled to grow in thankful, holy devotion to Him toward the day of glory.

The ascended Christ, through His servant Peter, is telling us that He bore our sins in His own body on the tree. We hear that by His grace, being made dead to sins and having the principle of new life in us, we are now called to live to righteousness. Submitting with all respect in the workplace is what the Christian should do, what the Christian is able to do, and what the Christian will do by the gracious power of God at work in him. In words of tremendous comfort and encouragement for us all—particularly for those suffering harsh injustice for doing good—Peter reminds us it is by Christ's wounds that we are healed. Bringing the words of Christ to us, Peter tenderly and honestly addresses our sin and reflects on the gracious work the Spirit accomplishes in us: we were like sheep going astray, but now we have returned to the Shepherd and Overseer of our souls. Amazing grace!

Do you see how all of this—God's call to holy living on the job, Jesus' perfect example, and His humble suffering for you—is to motivate you in the way you do your work at the shop, on the farm, at home, in college, or at the office? Do you see how a Christian, submitting on the job with all respect, is Christlike? We have been given profound motivation and full sufficiency in Jesus for all our needs. As the perfect Savior, He cleanses us from sin and enables us to die to the sins of disrespect and failure to submit. He empowers us to live in a new and holy way on the job, and works in us to will and to do His good pleasure. (Phil. 2:13) Through Jesus' wounds, we are healed. Even if your "master" expresses no gratitude for your respectful submission on the job, as you pursue this life in Christ your heavenly Father is honored and tells you so. We can steadily entrust ourselves to God through hard circumstances: He judges and will judge righteously.

The grace and glory of our God have been revealed to us in this precious Word. Take these verses, these blood-bought verses, with you: meditate on them, pray over them, and taste their sweetness, their incredible richness. Go to Christ, confessing your sin, worshipping Him, thanking Him for His great love and His willing submission for the sake of your salvation. And by the grace of God, go to work with the words of 1 Peter 1:18–25 emblazoned on your heart and mind, in thankful love for and confident faith in Him.

CHAPTER 7

Living Evangelistically: Biblical Motivation for Proclaiming the Gospel

Brian G. Najapfour with Josh Dear

Come now therefore, and I will send thee unto Pharaoh, that thou mayest bring forth my people the children of Israel out of Egypt. And Moses said unto God, Who am I, that I should go unto Pharaoh, and that I should bring forth the children of Israel out of Egypt? And he said, Certainly I will be with thee; and this shall be a token unto thee, that I have sent thee: When thou hast brought forth the people out of Egypt, ye shall serve God upon this mountain. And Moses said unto God, Behold, when I come unto the children of Israel, and shall say unto them, The God of your fathers hath sent me unto you; and they shall say to me, What is his name? what shall I say unto them? And God said unto Moses, I AM THAT I AM: and he said, Thus shalt thou say unto the children of Israel, I AM hath sent me unto you....

And Moses answered and said, But, behold, they will not believe me, nor hearken unto my voice: for they will say, The LORD hath not appeared unto thee. And the LORD said unto him, What is that in thine hand? And he said, A rod. And he said, Cast it on the ground. And he cast it on the ground, and it became a serpent; and Moses fled from before it. And the LORD said unto Moses, Put forth thine hand, and take it by the tail. And he put forth his hand, and caught it, and it became a rod in his hand: That they may believe that the LORD God of their fathers, the God of Abraham, the God of Isaac, and the God of Jacob, hath appeared unto thee....

And Moses said unto the LORD, O my LORD, I am not eloquent, neither heretofore, nor since thou hast spoken unto thy servant: but I am slow of speech, and of a slow tongue. And the LORD said unto him, Who hath made man's mouth? or who maketh the dumb, or deaf, or the seeing, or the blind? have not

I the LORD? Now therefore go, and I will be with thy mouth, and teach thee what thou shalt say. And he said, O my Lord, send, I pray thee, by the hand of him whom thou wilt send. And the anger of the LORD was kindled against Moses, and he said, Is not Aaron the Levite thy brother? I know that he can speak well. And also, behold, he cometh forth to meet thee: and when he seeth thee, he will be glad in his heart. And thou shalt speak unto him, and put words in his mouth: and I will be with thy mouth, and with his mouth, and will teach you what ye shall do. And he shall be thy spokesman unto the people: and he shall be, even he shall be to thee instead of a mouth, and thou shalt be to him instead of God. And thou shalt take this rod in thine hand, wherewith thou shalt do signs.

—Exodus 3:10–14; 4:1–5, 10–17

In this chapter, I will present five reasons we, as followers of Christ, must be actively engaging in evangelism and will respond to five excuses that are commonly used to avoid doing evangelism. I want to begin, however, by clarifying the meaning of two crucial terms.

First, what is evangelism? The term *evangelism* comes from the Greek word *euangelion*, meaning "gospel." So, to evangelize is simply to spread the gospel of the Lord Jesus Christ. For this reason, broadly speaking, anyone who faithfully announces the good news of Jesus Christ is an evangelist. In Acts 21:8, for example, Philip is identified as "the evangelist," although he is not an ordained minister, but rather a deacon. In this same way, all of us who are in Christ and are faithfully sharing the message of the cross with others are evangelists.

However, in the stricter sense, an evangelist is a divinely gifted person whose primary calling is to proclaim the gospel in places where it has not yet been proclaimed (Mark 16:15; Eph. 4:11). Acting as a missionary, a person who has been called by God to be an evangelist does not typically stay in one place, but moves on from one place to another in order to continue reaching the lost. In this chapter, I will use the term *evangelism* in its broader sense, as it refers to God's order that *every* Christian should be active in sharing the faith with others.

Second, what exactly is the gospel? We can answer this question easily by comparing two related passages of Scripture. In Mark 1:15, Jesus exhorts His listeners, "Repent ye, and believe the gospel," with the understood implication that, by doing so, they will be saved. However, in Acts 16:30–31, the Philippian jailer inquires of Paul and Silas, "Sirs, what must I do to be saved?" to which they reply, "Believe on the Lord Jesus Christ, and thou shalt be saved."

So, while Jesus teaches that people should "believe the gospel" in order to be saved, Paul and Silas instruct the jailer to "believe on the Lord Jesus" in order to be saved. Here we see that the expressions *the gospel* and *Jesus Christ* are essentially synonymous. The gospel *is* Jesus Christ; Jesus Christ *is* the gospel! Therefore, to proclaim the gospel is to proclaim Christ, and to reject the gospel is to reject Christ.

Of course, many Christians believe that the work of evangelism is only for pastors and those who are specifically called to be evangelists. They feel that as long as they are faithful members of a church and are serving Jesus in *some* way, then it's not really necessary for them to seek out people who are spiritually lost and attempt to talk to them about Jesus. After all, they may reason, God can save lost sinners in many different ways, with or without our personal participation in evangelism.

However, this is not the attitude that Scripture teaches us to have! Please allow me to offer five biblical reasons why *all* believers must evangelize.

Five Reasons All Believers Must Share the Gospel

First, evangelism is a way of life. In the book of Acts, evangelism is shown to be a regular practice among the believers in Christ. Acts 8:4 says, "Therefore they [believers] that were scattered abroad [because of persecution] went every where preaching the word." The Greek word that is translated here as "preaching" (*euangelizo*) can also be translated as "evangelizing" or "proclaiming the gospel." These persecuted believers were not ordained pastors, but whenever God gave them an opportunity, they shared the message of the cross with unbelievers—even in the midst of persecution! They evangelized wherever they went because they understood evangelism to be a vital part of their life in Christ. Evangelism was a way of life for them. As followers of Christ in our own day, we should follow their example of faithful Christian living and regard evangelism as a daily part of our lives, too.

Second, evangelism is the very essence of our identity. Evangelism is inextricably tied to our identity as God's people. Question 32 of the Heidelberg Catechism (1563) asks, "But why are you called a Christian?" and then answers, "Because by faith I am a member of Christ (Acts 11:26; 1 John 2:27) and thus a partaker of His anointing (Acts 2:17)."[1] Jesus, the Son of God, is ordained by the Father and anointed with His Spirit to be our chief Prophet, High Priest, and eternal King. In Christ, we become partakers of His anointing. That is, we become prophets, priests, and kings. Yes, if you are a Christian, you are also one of God's prophets! We are prophets in the sense that we proclaim Christ to others, and, as we have already observed, the proclamation of Christ is at the very heart of evangelism.

Truly, if we are in Christ, we *are* evangelists! We are publishers, proclaimers, and promoters of the good news! Commenting on the name *Jesus,* the apostle Peter says, "Neither is there salvation in any other: for there is none other name under heaven given among men, whereby we must be saved" (Acts 4:12). Wherever we go, we should remind ourselves of what we are in Christ—proclaimers of the gospel—and we should never be ashamed of this identity, which our loving Savior gives to us!

Third, evangelism arises from our love for unbelievers. Jesus commands us, "Thou shalt love thy neighbour as thyself" (Matt. 22:39). How can we say that we love our neighbors, especially our unbelieving neighbors, if we do not share the gospel with them?

If we were to see our neighbor's house burning in the middle of the night, how would we choose to express our love for him? Depending on the precise situation, calling "911" on his behalf might be the most helpful thing that we could do. If we were able, though, it might be even more helpful for us to run toward our neighbor's house and shout: "Hey, get out of your house! It's on fire!" In other words, if we are really concerned about the well-being of our neighbor, we will make every effort to give him our best help and to minister to his most urgent need.

Unbelievers are much like our neighbor in this illustration. (In fact, when Jesus shares the parable of the good Samaritan in Luke

---

1. The Heidelberg Catechism (1563), in *Reformed Confessions of the 16th and 17th Centuries in English Translation: Vol. 2, 1552–1566,* compiled with introductions by James T. Dennison (Grand Rapids: Reformation Heritage Books, 2010), 777.

10:29–37, He seems to strongly imply that lost people—as well as all other people whom God might put in our paths from day to day—*are* our neighbors.) If they remain unrepentant of their sins and disbelieving in Christ, they will suffer forever in the lake of fire. However, if we love them, as God repeatedly commands us to do, then we should feel *compelled* to share the gospel with them—and to help them understand that if they genuinely repent of their sins and believe in the Lord Jesus Christ, they will not perish in hell but have everlasting life in heaven. How loving are we if we do not share this information with the people around us?

Another helpful illustration is that of neighbors who are dying of cancer. We have knowledge of the cure that can save them. In this situation, would we allow shyness, fear, or perhaps even apathy to prevent us from telling them about the cure? No. Likewise, should we allow anything to prevent us from telling unbelievers about Jesus. If so, we would be disobeying God's Word and dishonoring God Himself. Yet this is precisely the situation that we *are* currently in with regard to the gospel, which has been entrusted to us for both *keeping* (guarding against attack and misrepresentation) and *sharing* (1 Thess. 2:4; 2 Tim. 1:12–14; etc.).

Just as we could never in good conscience allow our neighbors to die from a house fire about which we can warn them or from a disease for which we have the cure, so we should not let them pass from this life without hearing some proclamation of the gospel of Christ! If we genuinely care for those who are lost, we will surely pray for their salvation and try our best to help them see that they are perishing without Christ. A love for our "neighbor" compels us to do this.

Fourth, evangelism originates in the very nature of our God. Praise be to God, for He *is* an evangelist! The very essence of God's love is demonstrated to us in this way, for as 1 John 4:10 reminds us, "Herein is love, not that we loved God, but that he loved us, and sent his Son to be the propitiation for our sins." Without God loving us and pursuing us in such a way, we would all be destined for hell! Yet God loves us and takes the initiative to draw many lost sinners to Himself, so that, in Christ, we may be eternally saved.

In Luke 2:10–11, God's angel (or heavenly messenger) evangelizes the shepherds on God's behalf, saying: "Fear not: for, behold, I bring you good tidings of great joy, which shall be to all people. For unto you is born this day in the city of David a Saviour, which is Christ the Lord." So when we evangelize, we imitate God, who created us, loves us, and commands us to grow increasingly into the likeness of His Son. In fact, the only reason that we are even able to evangelize is because God evangelized us first! Therefore, it's a tremendous honor and blessing that God invites us to be a part of His saving work here on earth—and we should not neglect this invitation to honor Him by telling others about His love.

Since evangelism *begins* with God Himself, though, we should also acknowledge that it *ends* with Him, too! In other words, it is actually God who saves people—not we. After all, can we—in our limited abilities—save the people around us from eternal judgment? Absolutely not! God alone accomplishes salvation as He sovereignly elects those who are to be saved and draws people to Himself through the power of the Holy Spirit. Nonetheless, God has chosen to use us—and especially our preaching and sharing of His unchanging Word—to bring this to pass. Though God does not tell us in advance whom He will ultimately save, He instructs us to share His good news with all people and to be faithful in evangelizing, knowing that only He can truly accomplish salvation in the hearts of lost sinners.

Fifth, evangelism is a command set forth in the Great Commission. Consider the familiar but profoundly significant instructions of our Lord in Matthew 28:18–20: "And Jesus came and spake unto them, saying, All power is given unto me in heaven and in earth. Go ye therefore, and teach all nations, baptizing them in the name of the Father, and of the Son, and of the Holy Ghost: teaching them to observe all things whatsoever I have commanded you: and, lo, I am with you alway, even unto the end of the world. Amen."

We cannot make *disciples* (as the ESV translates it), who are healthy and growing followers of Christ, unless we first proclaim the gospel to them. The parallel passage in Mark 16:15 makes this clear by instructing us to "Go ye into all the world, and *preach the gospel* to every creature" (italics added). Evangelism is the crucial first step in making disciples for Christ, for people cannot fruitfully grow in their understanding of God's Word until they first encounter the God who so lovingly gave that Word to us. Therefore, we must evangelize on a regular basis if we are to obey Christ's command to us in the Great Commission.

Evangelism is not something that should cause us to boast, though—God fully expects us to evangelize in obedience to Him. Paul writes, "For though I preach the gospel, I have nothing to glory of: for necessity is laid upon me; yea, woe is unto me, if I preach not the gospel!" (1 Cor. 9:16). Likewise, he writes in Romans 1:14–15: "I am debtor both to the Greeks, and to the Barbarians; both to the wise, and to the unwise. So, as much as in me is, I am ready to preach the gospel to you that are at Rome also." Paul recognizes how God has worked through others to help him in his own faith journey, and he concludes that, ultimately, it is God to whom all credit is due in regard to salvation, since God alone is the Author and Perfecter of our faith. In agreeing to preach the gospel in Rome, where the church was already firmly established, Paul is also acknowledging that the gospel is not merely for the lost who need to be saved, but also for growing Christians who need to be freshly encouraged in their devotion to Christ.

Priscilla J. Owens (1829–1907) wrote a beautiful hymn that we still love to sing in our churches; it is titled "Jesus Saves" (also known as "We Have Heard the Joyful Sound"). The lyrics serve to remind us of our all-important task as Christians:

We have heard the joyful sound: Jesus saves! Jesus saves!
Spread the tidings all around: Jesus saves! Jesus saves!
Bear the news to every land, climb the mountains, cross the waves;
Onward! 'tis our Lord's command; Jesus saves! Jesus saves![2]

Nevertheless, please notice that this point about evangelism being a divine command for us to obey is placed last in my list, though we might be tempted to place it first. While it's crucial for us to remember that God does, indeed, *command* us to share the gospel, I placed it last here for a very specific reason—I don't want you to share the gospel out of *guilt*, but out of *gratitude* for what God has done for you in Jesus Christ. We are never to proclaim God's message of love and salvation as militant soldiers simply doing what's demanded of us. Instead, it should be out of love for God and love for our neighbor that we eagerly, prayerfully, and joyfully seek out opportunities to share the good news with others.

---

2. Priscilla J. Owens, "Jesus Saves," 1882; www.hymntime.com/tch/htm/j/e/s/ jesussav.htm (accessed December 13, 2013).

If a husband were to bring home flowers, chocolates, and a beautiful card for his wife, would it matter if he later confessed to buying these things for her out of duty—in order to simply *obey* what God's Word commands that he do as a husband? Yes, it would matter! The wife's desire is not simply to receive tangible gifts from her husband, but—far more important—to know that whatever gifts he might give to her are given because he loves her, cherishes her, and wants to express his delight in her and his gratitude for all that she means to him. In the same way, we should not evangelize out of a sense of guilt or duty, which doesn't honor God in the appropriate way, but out of our genuine love for God, our joy in knowing Him, our gratitude for the multitude of ways that He blesses our lives each day, and our deep desire that other people might come to know Him as we have.

We should remember another beloved hymn that expresses these convictions so well—"I Love to Tell the Story"—and allow these lyrics by Katherine Hankey (1834–1911) to inspire our hearts:

> I love to tell the story, because I know 'tis true;
> It satisfies my longings as nothing else can do.[3]

In other words, she is evangelizing because it satisfies her longings and brings her delight.

Evangelism brings joy to the faithful Christian, but it also brings joy to the angels in heaven and to our triune God whenever we do this! Please ask yourself: When was the last time you experienced this kind of joy, the joy that flows out of the work of evangelism? We are so happy when we get married and when we have children, and we can't wait to tell others about these good things that have happened to us. But what about the happiness that should come from our relationship to God? Do we have the same zeal for sharing about God's love? We should!

The hymn continues:

> I love to tell the story, it did so much for me;
> And that is just the reason I tell it now to thee.[4]

All of us who are children of God should be able to echo these sentiments in our hearts as we reflect on how knowing God has

---

3. Katherine Hankey, "I Love to Tell the Story," 1866; www.hymnsite.com/lyrics/umh156.sht (accessed December 13, 2013).

4. Hankey, "I Love to Tell the Story."

changed our lives in significant ways. The gospel has done so much for us; Jesus has done so much for us! Christ gave His life for us; He died on the cross to save us from the power and penalty of sin. We should have been in hell a long time ago, but here we are, still alive and now free from the bondage of sin. He has done *so much* for us, and that should be more than enough to motivate us to evangelize— not out of guilt, but out of love.

Of course, we all have excuses for not evangelizing; we all come up with legitimate-sounding alibis to justify our failure to tell others about Christ. In fact, I'm going to "help you" in your excuse-making by returning to Exodus 3–4 and offering five popular reasons that believers often give for not evangelizing. At the same time, though, I'm going to share what I believe are God's answers to our alibis, which I hope will help us to see the foolishness of our excuses and to recognize our need to evangelize in spite of them.

Five Excuses for Not Evangelizing

1. *Who am I?* When God commands Moses to go before Pharaoh, the first excuse, which Moses offers in the form of a question, is: "Who am I, that I should go unto Pharaoh, and that I should bring forth the children of Israel out of Egypt?" (Ex. 3:11). Today, we often express this same concern, saying, "I know that I'm supposed to share the gospel, but *who am I* to do this?"

Perhaps what Moses is saying here is this: "Why are you sending *me*? I am weak, and I am already eighty years old, but you are sending me to Pharaoh, who is strong. You want *me* to go to *him*?" Notice, however, what God tells Moses in verse 12: "I will be with thee." What a beautiful promise! God is telling Moses, "Yes, I know that you're old, and yes, I know that you're weak, but *I* will be with you!"

You might be using this excuse today. Perhaps you're saying, "I am shy"; "I am weak"; "I have no formal theological training"; or "I am afraid," and you're still asking God, "Who am I that you would send me out to evangelize?" But remember what Jesus tells us in Matthew 28:20: "Lo, I am with you alway, even unto the end of the world." We don't do the work of evangelism alone and in our own strength. God is with us!

David Livingstone (1813–1873), a Scottish missionary who traveled to Africa and helped open one-third of the continent to Christian missions, came to cherish Matthew 28:20 as his "life verse." After some difficult years of ministry in Africa, he returned to Scotland to share publicly about the ministry that he'd done. When he was asked whether he would be willing to return to Africa to do additional work, he offered the following reply: "Would you like me to tell you what supported me through all the years of exile among people whose language I could not understand, and whose attitude towards me was always uncertain and often hostile? It was this: *'Lo, I am with you alway, even unto the end of the world!'* On those words I staked everything, and they never failed!"[5]

Livingstone found comfort in this verse, knowing that he could go wherever the Lord led him because *the Lord would always be with him.* In the same way, God is with us, too—not just some of the time, but *all* the time! So be comforted, and know that whenever we set out to do the Lord's work, He goes with us as our guide and our comfort in all that we do.

Your concern may be, "I'm not well educated," but you don't have to be a scholar to share your faith, for the God who knows *all* things goes with you! Consider also the account in Acts 4, where we see that Peter and John are preaching the gospel and leading thousands of people to Christ, but the skeptical religious leaders confront them and ask where their power and authority to do this comes from. After they explain that Jesus, who has been raised from the dead, is their authority, the leaders are amazed. Note their reaction in verse 13: "Now when they saw the boldness of Peter and John, and perceived that they were unlearned and ignorant men, they marvelled; and they took knowledge of them, that they had been with Jesus." Peter and John were not well-educated men, yet God used that lack of learning to demonstrate His power. In the same way, God can use each of us to spread the message of the cross in spite of our particular shortcomings, and He promises to be *with us* as we serve Him.

2. *What shall I say to them?* This excuse is used in Exodus 3:13: "And Moses said unto God, Behold, when I come unto the children of Israel, and shall say unto them, The God of your fathers hath sent me unto you; and they shall say to me, What is his name? what

---

5. David Livingstone, cited in F. W. Boreham, "David Livingstone's Life Text"; www.wholesomewords.org/missions/bliving8.html (accessed December 13, 2013).

shall I say unto them?" Please notice that while Moses' first concern is about defending himself to Pharaoh, this second excuse is regarding his ability to establish his authority with the Israelites themselves. Moses is contemplating his interaction with various people—the Egyptian ruler whose authority he will be challenging as well as the people of God whom he's being called to rescue. Like us, Moses tries to consider every potential problem with the call God has given to him!

The question is one with which we can easily identify: "What shall I say?" In other words, if the people to whom we are sent start asking us questions about God, inquiring as to whether we truly know Him and represent Him, what can we say to demonstrate that we *do*? Our knowledge of God and His Word is insufficient in itself, so what answer can we possibly offer to establish such lofty credentials—that we have been sent by Almighty God?

In Moses' case, the answer is given—again—in the verse that follows: "And God said unto Moses, I AM THAT I AM: and he said, Thus shalt thou say unto the children of Israel, I AM hath sent me unto you" (Ex. 3:14). In identifying Himself as "I AM," God is reminding us that He is the faithful, covenant-keeping God who does not change. God always has been and always will be, and His Word is true today, just as it has always been true. Therefore, we can fully trust in Him as He guides us, knowing that all that He says is true and that future events will come to pass according to His sovereign plan.

One of the reasons we try so hard to avoid evangelism is that we want to make the gospel more complicated than it actually is. The gospel is simple! We should learn this lesson from the example of Paul and Silas, who—as we've already mentioned—tell the Philippian jailer, "Believe on the Lord Jesus Christ, and thou shalt be saved" (Acts 16:31). There's no mention here of the two disciples insisting that the jailer learn the five points of Calvinism or subscribe to the Westminster Confession of Faith (helpful though those two statements of faith are). No, Paul and Silas simply tell him that if he will believe on the Lord Jesus Christ he will be saved. *That* is the gospel message.

We can also learn this lesson directly from our Lord's example. When the thief on the cross speaks to Jesus and petitions, "Lord, remember me when thou comest into thy kingdom" (Luke 23:42),

Jesus does not correct him by saying, "I'm sorry, but you must specifically say, 'Lord, save me from the power and penalty of my sin,' or I won't be able to do anything for you." Jesus never corrects him, because He knows precisely what the thief is asking. Jesus simply responds, "To day shalt thou be with me in paradise" (v. 43).

In evangelism, we are simply announcing the good news—we are not lecturing; we are not teaching "systematic theology"; we are not expounding on the doctrine of "irresistible grace"; and we are certainly not trying to discern for ourselves whether or not the person is one of the elect of God. Please do not do that when evangelizing! Instead, use the approach that Paul and Silas used—simply tell people that if they will believe on the Lord Jesus Christ, they *will* be saved! Why? Because that is what God calls us to do as we share the gospel with lost people and because the power of conviction comes not from our ability to persuade, but from God Himself and from His gospel message. That is why, in Romans 1:16, Paul writes, "For I am not ashamed of the gospel of Christ: for it is the power of God unto salvation to every one that believeth."

Sometimes, in evangelism, all you really need to do is quote a passage from the Bible and pray that God will use that verse to transform the life of the hearer. In 1857, Charles Spurgeon (1834–1892) was asked to preach a message at the Crystal Palace. A day or two before preaching there, Spurgeon went to visit the building in order to test the acoustics of the room and determine where the preaching platform should be. To do this, he simply stood before the seemingly empty room and cried in a loud voice, "Behold the Lamb of God, which taketh away the sin of the world" (John 1:29). Spurgeon later learned that a workman who was in one of the galleries that day heard these words proclaimed, came under the conviction of sin, went home that evening, and surrendered his life to the Lord—simply because of hearing Spurgeon cry out a single verse of Scripture![6]

Truly, there's no limit to how God can work miracles from our humble obedience to Him. Don't be discouraged if you haven't formally studied theology. If you know John 3:16, then you have the message! If you know Romans 6:23, then you have the message! You

---

6. Cited in "Great Story Illustrating That God Moves In A Mysterious Way, His Wonders To Perform!"; www.gospelweb.net/AngelStories/BeholdTheLambOfGod .htm (accessed December 13, 2013).

don't need to be a theologian or an apologist in order to share your faith. The gospel is simple, and we are to keep it simple when we share it with others.

3. *They will not believe me.* Exodus 4:1 states, "And Moses answered and said, But, behold, they will not believe me, nor hearken unto my voice; for they will say, The LORD hath not appeared unto thee." God's kindness in responding to this protest is a tremendous demonstration of His grace and mercy toward Moses—and toward us—for it is a direct contradiction of what God has already declared to be true. In Exodus 3:18, God had explained to Moses, "They shall hearken to thy voice." Yet with his very next words, Moses expresses his unbelief in what God had just said! Rather than responding in righteous anger, however, the Lord graciously offers Moses a quick demonstration of His miracle-working power (Ex. 4:2–9), so as to give him assurance that, even in the face of opposition among the Egyptians, God's miracles will substantiate the words that Moses is to speak.

In raising this concern, Moses is essentially saying, "Lord, now I know that Thou wilt be with me and I know what I should say, but the people to whom Thou art sending me *still* won't believe me." This makes me want to say to Moses: "Have you even *tried* it yet? God clearly told you what to do, and even though you haven't even tried it yet, you're convinced that the people won't listen to you! Try it first. You're so pessimistic!"

I'm afraid that, just like Moses, we, too, are pessimistic about simply going where God sends us. We have a never-ending list of worries, fears, and "What if…" questions, and we let them keep us from doing God's will. Sometimes we say things like, "I don't want to talk to my nonbelieving neighbors about Jesus because they won't believe what I tell them." Again, when I hear believers say that, I want to ask, "Have you tried it yet?"

We should first *go* where God sends and *do* as He has instructed. Then, if the people still don't believe us, so what? Our faithfulness is determined by our obedience to God's commands, and nothing more. It is not our duty to make others believe the gospel; that is the work of the Holy Spirit! We might wish that we *could* make others believe in Christ, for their own benefit and blessing, but we don't have that ability. Our duty is simply to tell them about Jesus Christ.

The people to whom God sends us might have a lot of questions for us. If so, we can help them find the answers that they seek in God's Word. However, we should also remember the old English proverb: "You can lead a horse to water, but you can't make him drink." You cannot force an unbeliever to drink from the fountain of life, but you can lead that person to the living water and ask the Holy Spirit to move him or her to come to Jesus Christ and be saved.

We can also attempt to create a thirst for the gospel by first establishing a genuine friendship with a lost person and then, at the most appropriate time, sharing our personal testimony of faith in Christ. If the other person should ask, "Why are you showing this care and concern for me?" that is the perfect opportunity to say, "Because the Bible says to love your neighbor as yourself, and I want to share this love that I've found in Jesus Christ, so that you can experience it for yourself."

Again, it is God's work to make people believe in Him, but we have the responsibility to share the gospel with others. That's why, in these passages in Exodus, we see the balance between divine sovereignty and human responsibility. Admittedly, some believers try to use God's sovereignty as an excuse for not evangelizing, saying: "I am a strong believer in God's sovereignty and in election, and I know that the Bible tells us (in Eph. 1:4) that before the foundation of the world God chose some to be saved. So, I trust that, in His time, God will bring some of those elect believers to our church."

Oh, my friend, you are dead wrong if you think like this! This is the problem with hyper-Calvinism—it emphasizes the sovereignty of God to the extreme, leading to a complete denial of our God-ordained responsibility as His people. On August 1, 1858, Spurgeon preached a sermon titled, "Sovereign Grace and Man's Responsibility," in which he said: "You ask me to reconcile the two [i.e. divine sovereignty and human responsibility]. I answer, they do not want any reconcilement; I never tried to reconcile them to myself, because I could never see a discrepancy.... Both are true; no two truths can be inconsistent with each other; and what you have to do is to believe them both."[7] Spurgeon recognized—as we should—that while we cannot save anyone in our own limited abilities (not even ourselves!),

---

7. Charles Spurgeon, "Sovereign Grace and Man's Responsibility," www.spurgeon.org/sermons/0207.htm (accessed December 13, 2013).

God has nonetheless chosen to use us to proclaim the gospel throughout the world. What an honor it is that God invites us to participate in the building of His kingdom on earth, and how foolish we would be to neglect such a blessed opportunity!

Some people believe that the doctrine of election is an enemy of biblical evangelism, but it is not. In fact, it is our encouragement as we evangelize! If there were no election, there would be no guarantee for us that spiritually dead sinners could ever be made new in Christ. The fact that God chose to save *some* from before the foundation of the world should motivate us to go out and reach the lost, knowing that some people will surely be saved!

Our job, however, is not to attempt to recognize the elect from the non-elect—as if we are even able to do so—but to proclaim the gospel to all lost sinners and to pray for their salvation, trusting in God to save those whom He chooses to save. Even Jesus proclaims the gospel in this way, inviting all who hear Him to respond in faith. Jesus addresses a large and diverse crowd of people, saying, "Come unto me, all ye that labour and are heavy laden, and I will give you rest" (Matt. 11:28). Jesus knows (as He states in John 6:44) that only those whom the Father draws will ever respond to His call, but that does not prevent Him from calling all people to repent and trust in Him. We must learn from the example set by our Lord—the gospel is to be proclaimed to *all* people, and it's to be shared faithfully, with the understanding that only God Himself is truly able to save!

4. *I am not eloquent.* Moses uses this excuse in Exodus 4:10: "And Moses said unto the LORD, O my Lord, I am not eloquent, neither heretofore, nor since thou hast spoken unto thy servant: but I am slow of speech, and of a slow tongue." Who is eloquent in speech? I certainly am not! Thankfully, though, the power of God does not depend on our eloquence. In trying to communicate the gospel to others, we may stumble over some words or commit some grammatical errors along the way, but so be it! We serve a sovereign God who can overcome our mistakes—or perhaps even *use* our mistakes to accomplish His eternal purpose and plan.

Many people claim that they are so nervous at the thought of evangelism that they don't believe they would even be able to communicate clearly while sharing the gospel with a lost person. If this describes you, please consider how you would respond if you saw one of your children drowning in a pool. Would you argue that you were so nervous that you couldn't articulate words, or would you anxiously scream at the top of your voice, "Please, somebody, save my child!"? Undoubtedly, in a situation like this, you would not care about your speaking skills; you probably would not even care a great deal about your life. Most likely, your only concern in that moment would be for the child who was dying and urgently needed to be saved.

Of course, this serves to illustrate the evangelistic process, as well. All around us, people are dying without knowing Christ and are being condemned to an eternity in hell, permanently separated from the love, peace, joy, and comfort that can be found only in God. Do we care that these people are perishing in such a way? We certainly should! There's little doubt, though, that one of the main reasons we don't evangelize is that we simply don't care about others—certainly not to the degree that Scripture tells us to.

We think of our families as well as ourselves, but we fall tragically short in our concern for the people to whom we aren't related, and we are even less concerned about those we do not personally know. Yet, according to Scripture, every person who dies outside of Christ will experience God's wrath in hell forever. Therefore, we should take time to contemplate the biblical teaching about hell and allow this disturbing reality to give us a greater concern for those who are lost. It should also inspire us in our prayers for the salvation of others and in our evangelism.

After Moses expresses his concerns about his poor speaking skills, God provides the following response: "Who hath made man's mouth? or who maketh the dumb, or deaf, or the seeing, or the blind? Have not I the LORD? Now therefore go, and I will be with thy mouth, and teach thee what thou shalt say" (Ex. 4:11–12).

Jesus offers similar counsel to His disciples: "And when they bring you unto the synagogues, and unto magistrates, and powers, take ye no thought how or what thing ye shall answer, or what ye shall say: for the Holy Ghost shall teach you in the same hour what ye ought to say" (Luke 12:11–12).

At many times in my life, I have experienced God working in this way. On one occasion, I was sharing my faith with an atheist who had many questions for me, and I was amazed that, by God's grace, I was able to answer his questions. At the end of our conversation, I was surprised by how the Lord had guided both my thinking and my speech, enabling me to provide the right answers in the midst of that challenging conversation. Surely that was not me—it was the Holy Spirit working in me because of the grace of God. However, that's how God operates in our lives when we trust Him not only to guide us but also to equip us for all that He sends us to do.

In 1 Corinthians 2:1–4, Paul reminds us yet again that eloquent speech is not a prerequisite for serving Christ:

> And I, brethren, when I came to you, came not with excellency of speech or of wisdom, declaring unto you the testimony of God. For I determined not to know any thing among you, save Jesus Christ, and him crucified. And I was with you in weakness, and in fear, and in much trembling. And my speech and my preaching was not with enticing words of man's wisdom, but in demonstration of the Spirit and of power.

How encouraging it should be to all of us to know that God can work through us regardless of our imperfections! A popular quote declares, "An evangelist is a nobody who is seeking to tell everybody about Somebody who can help change anybody."[8] So, as God's humble "nobodies," each of us should remember that it is not our eloquence that can bring about lasting change in a lost person's life; rather, it is our all-powerful God working through the gospel message that we are all called to share.

5. *Please send someone else.* Exodus 4:13 states, "And he said, O my Lord, send, I pray thee, by the hand of him whom thou wilt send." Now we know why Moses has been making all of these excuses to the Lord—he simply does not want to go. Isn't the same true for us? We don't want to evangelize because we don't want to evangelize— and when we don't want to evangelize, we come up with alibis or reasons that we shouldn't have to serve the Lord in this way. Of course, we might be too embarrassed to admit this, but this is the reality for many Christians today, and—apparently—it was reality for Moses, too!

---

8. Cited in Roy B. Zuck, *The Speaker's Quote Book* (Grand Rapids: Kregel, 1997), 133.

When Moses makes this final effort to avoid doing what God has commanded him to do, Exodus 4:14 records that "the anger of the LORD was kindled against Moses." Oh, dear friends, let us not wait for the Lord to become angry with us because we make excuse upon excuse! Instead, let us go where He sends, willingly and lovingly, knowing that He will be with us, guiding us and enabling us to serve Him faithfully. In this case, God graciously provides Moses with a helper in the person of Aaron, his brother. As we go out to serve the Lord, though, we have the added blessing of knowing that the Holy Spirit, who is a far better helper, goes with us—guiding us, convicting us, and bringing us the peace of God even in the midst of our most difficult experiences.

Conclusion

In the event that any unbelievers have found their way to this chapter, your greatest need is to hear and respond to the gospel! You must believe in the Lord Jesus Christ—you must be saved! If you do not surrender your life fully to God, you will surely be separated from Him for all eternity in a very real and terrible place called hell.

However, you might say: "I want to turn to Christ, but how can I with all of the sin in my life? I simply don't have the ability to come to Jesus by faith." Consider Jesus' visit with a man who has been sick for thirty-eight years, recorded for us in John 5:8–9: "Jesus saith unto him, Rise, take up thy bed, and walk. And immediately the man was made whole, and took up his bed, and walked."

Notice here that the sick man does not question what Jesus is telling him to do. He does not say: "Are you okay? Don't you see that I can't walk?" On the contrary, he is immediately made whole and responds in obedience to what Jesus has said.

Let me suggest that, when we do evangelism, this is essentially what we are doing, too. We are sharing the gospel with people who are spiritually dead because of the sin in their lives, people who cannot save themselves. How, then, will they believe the gospel if they're still lost in sin? In their own abilities, they are unable to respond to the gospel—just as the sick man did not possess the ability to walk or to bring about his own healing.

Here is the beauty of the gospel: when Jesus says, "Come to Me," He gives you feet so that you can! When Jesus says, "Believe in Me,"

He gives you the faith to do so! This way, in the end, you always give *all* of the praise and glory to God. So please don't let anything keep you from surrendering your life to Christ, for as He calls you, He will also enable you to respond to His call and become a part of His eternal family.

Finally, to you who already belong to Christ (praise the Lord for that!), please stop making excuses for not sharing the gospel. Instead, establish better habits of talking to others about Jesus on a daily basis and presenting the gospel to those who are lost whenever you see an opportunity to do so. Also, pray along with the hymn writer Herbert G. Tovey (1888–1972) the lyrics to his great song, titled "A Passion for Souls":

> Give me a passion for souls, dear Lord,
> A passion to save the lost…
> Jesus, I long, I long to be winning
> Men who are lost, and constantly sinning;
> O may this hour be one of beginning
> The story of pardon to tell.[9]

Learn to pray with George Whitefield, an English evangelist: "O Lord, give me souls or take my soul!"[10]

Also, make time to read some good Christian books on the topic of evangelism and some good biographies of missionaries and evangelists that might inspire you in your own evangelistic endeavors.

Let me conclude this chapter with an illustration that I heard several years ago, while I was in the Philippines. A little boy who had gone with his family to a family camp got lost in the forest. Though the family members and other people looked everywhere for him, they could not find him. After hours of searching, everyone returned to the camp, overwhelmed with disappointment. Then someone suggested that they work their way back through the forest holding hands with one another, so as not to miss any area. They did this and soon found the boy, but it was too late. He was already dead. If only they had worked together in this way sooner, then—humanly speaking—they might have been able to save the boy's life.

---

9. Herbert G. Tovey, "A Passion for Souls"; www.hymntime.com/tch/htm/g/i/v/ givemeap.htm (accessed December 13, 2013).

10. George Whitefield, cited in Zuck, *The Speaker's Quote Book*, 359.

Dear friends, this is what we need to do, too, as we seek to reach the lost who are perishing in their sins. I encourage you to spiritually hold the hand of your pastor, your elders, and your fellow church members. Let's hold hands together and proclaim the gospel of the Lord Jesus Christ in hopes that many who are dead will soon be made alive in Christ by the power of the gospel!

CHRISTIAN LIVING IN ITS
EARTHLY STORMS

CHAPTER 8

Living in the Furnace of Affliction

Gerald Bilkes

For the Christian, life is made up of both prosperity and adversity.[1] The Preacher says: "In the day of prosperity be joyful, but in the day of adversity consider: God also hath set the one over against the other, to the end that man should find nothing after him" (Eccl. 7:14). All Christians are at some point on the continuum of prosperity and adversity. And all Christians at one time or another experience both prosperity and adversity. For those in adversity, even extreme adversity, the Bible reveals a glorious comfort. And for those in prosperity, even extreme prosperity, the Bible prepares them for the days of affliction, which will come in God's time. Whether in adversity or prosperity, we ought to remember the words of the Zurich Reformer Otho Wermullerus: "As long as we are upon the earth we are, as it were, in a camp of siege, where we must ever be skirmishing and fighting, and know neither who shall break out and give the onset against us, nor how, nor when."[2]

Often, those who have suffered much affliction are the greatest teachers of suffering well. One of the great hallmarks of the apostolic church was the grace they had to suffer well. The blood of unflinching martyrs was one of the most powerful factors in the growth of the church. As Tertullian wrote, "The oftener we are mown down by

---

1. I would like to thank Michael Borg, my research assistant, for his work on this chapter.

2. Otho Wermullerus, *Most Precious Pearl, Teaching All Men to Love and Embrace the Cross, as a Most Sweet and Necessary Thing Unto the Soul*, trans. Miles Coverdale (London: James Nisbet and Co., 1838), 129.

you, the more in number we grow; the blood of Christians is seed."[3] As they faced martyrdom, the observation of many was "these people die well." The suffering of the prophets, apostles, martyrs, and saints can be used to instruct future generations to follow the Lord in adversity, persecution, and affliction.

For this reason, one can also learn great things from the English Puritans. They suffered religious and civil persecutions, such as being put out of their churches, losing their livelihoods in the infamous Great Ejection[4] and Five Mile Act,[5] and even losing their lives, as among the Scottish Puritans during the Killing Times in Scotland.[6] They suffered natural persecutions in a time when both infant and general mortality rates were very high; diseases, plagues, and other calamities were rampant. They suffered internal afflictions, with a keen sense of their sins, the buffetings of Satan, and various temptations. Their often-steadfast resolution in spite of all these adversities makes them excellent examples as to how to suffer well.[7]

When theology is formed in the difficulties of affliction, doctrine is not merely rational. Rather, theology becomes more relevant, arguments more credible, and commentaries more applicable—the study

---

3. Tertullian, *Apology,* trans. S. Thelwall, ch. 50, in *Ante-Nicene Fathers,* ed. Alexander Robert and James Donaldson (New York: Charles Scribner's Sons, 1918), 3:55.

4. See, for example, Gary Brady, *The Great Ejection* (Darlington, U.K.: Evangelical Press, 2012).

5. See, for example, Samuel Rawson Gardiner, *A Student's History of England: From the Earliest Times to the Death of Queen Victoria,* vol. 2 (London: Longmans, Green, and Co., 1907), 590.

6. Peter Hume Brown, *History of Scotland,* vol. 2 (London: Cambridge University Press, 1911), 335ff.

7. The Puritans wrote many practical works on suffering; see, for example: Thomas Boston, *The Crook in the Lot* (Glasgow: Porteous and Hislop, 1863); David Brainerd, "Life and Diary of the Rev. David Brainerd," in *The Works of Jonathan Edwards,* vol. 2 (Peabody, Mass.: Hendrickson, 2003), 313–458; William Bridge, "A Lifting Up the Downcast," in *The Works of the Rev. William Bridge,* vol. 2 (London: Thomas Tegg, 1845), 3–282; Jeremiah Burroughs, *The Rare Jewel of Christian Contentment* (reprint, Edinburgh: Banner of Truth, 2005); John Flavel, *Divine Conduct or The Mystery of Providence* (London: L.B. Seeley and Son, 1824); Samuel Rutherford, *The Trial and Triumph of Faith: Lessons from Christ's Gracious Answers to a Woman Whose Faith Would Not Give Up* (Edinburgh: Banner of Truth, 2001); Richard Sibbes, *The Bruised Reed* (Edinburgh: Banner of Truth, 1998); Joseph Symond, *The Case and Cure of a Deserted Soul: Or a Treatise Concerning the Nature, Kinds, Degrees, Symptoms, Causes, Cure of, and Mistakes About Spiritual Desertions* (Morgan, Pa.: Soli Deo Gloria, 1997); and Thomas Watson, *All Things for Good* (Edinburgh: Banner of Truth, 1986).

of God becomes affective. The Puritans' experience of suffering emboldened them to *confess* the faith more purely and enabled them to *convey* it more pastorally and persuasively. As George Swinnock wrote: "A sanctified person, like a silver bell, the harder he is smitten, the better he sounds."[8] And those who suffer well, encourage well.

In this way, the Puritans reflected the scriptural doctrine of suffering. As they pored over, expounded, and understood what the Bible says about suffering, they sought to resemble the encouragement of the Bible: "Comfort ye, comfort ye my people" (Isa. 40:1). Biblically speaking, every affliction gives an opportunity for men and women to experience the resurrecting power of God (cf. 2 Cor. 1:8–11), and so the Scriptures, rightly perceived, give us direction on how to suffer well.

In this vein, the apostle Peter so encourages his readers in the first epistle: "Beloved, think it not strange concerning the fiery trial which is to try you, as though some strange thing happened unto you; but rejoice, inasmuch as ye are partakers of Christ's sufferings; that, when his glory shall be revealed, ye may be glad also with exceeding joy" (1 Peter 4:12–13).

The significance of this passage lies in the phrase "think it not strange." The Greek means "let it not be strange to you."[9] Peter essentially leads his readers by the hand, taking them through a tour of the furnace of affliction. In this way, Peter prepares his readers, so that when affliction comes, they will not be incited to think that it is strange, unexpected, useless, or inappropriate for a faithful follower of Christ. Similarly, when we suffer, we are often inclined to think that something is going horribly wrong. "No," Peter says. "Do not think that way. The fiery trial is not a strange or wrong place." So he lifts the veil on what is so often a mystery to believers—the reason and purpose of sufferings. In this chapter, we want to unpack Peter's instruction regarding the suffering of believers, looking at ten reasons why we should not regard the furnace as strange.

The Name

First, the fiery trial should not seem strange because of the name Scripture gives it. Giving a name to something entails a sense of familiarity or

---

8. George Swinnock, *The Works of George Swinnock* (Edinburgh: James Nichol, 1863), 3:404.

9. The Greek is *xenizoo*, from which we get the word *xenophobia*.

connection. Things that are named are things personally known. Brilliantly, Peter uses the term "fiery trial" (4:12). He anticipated this concept in 1:7: "The trial of your faith, being much more precious than of gold that perisheth, though it be tried with fire, might be found unto praise and honour and glory at the appearing of Jesus Christ."

In 4:12, the Greek uses two nouns: *fire* and *trial*. First, "the fire" (*ho purosis*) relates that Peter is being honest about the difficulty and intensity of the trial. Fire is hot. Fire burns. Fire consumes. Second, "trial" (*peirasmos*) shows that this fire is merely temporary. Also, a trial serves the good purpose of testing for truth. We would not willingly choose these things for ourselves—trying, difficult, and intense temporary trials meant to evaluate our very hearts.

"Fiery trial" forms the graphic picture of a furnace.[10] Peter is referring to the ancient trade and skill of refining ore. The refiner would heat a kiln, put the ore on a lever into the smelting chamber, and watch and wait until the ore was molten and the dross or impurities separated from the metal. Often, the refiner would put air into the metal to remove the layer of dross at the top or would skim it off with a sharp tool. He would continue this process of removing the dross until all the impurities had been removed. One small miscalculation or a failure to remove even trace amounts of impurities would make the ore less refined, and therefore less valuable. This process would occur a number of times until the ore was exactly as he desired it. It was common practice to think that refinement was complete when the refiner could see his own clear reflection in the metal.

But what exactly is Peter naming here? What is this fire, this trial, this furnace?[11] Taking the whole of Scripture together, we can distinguish three aspects to the fiery trial of which Peter speaks.

---

10. Cf. Joel Green, *1 Peter*, Two Horizons New Testament Commentary (Grand Rapids: Eerdmans, 2007), 148.

11. Some have argued for a historical understanding of "fiery trial" as the persecutions of the Roman emperors; see Green, *1 Peter*, 8ff., and Gerald L. Borcher, "The Conduct of Christians in the Face of the 'Fiery Ordeal' (4:12–5:11)," *Review and Expositor* 79 (1982): 451–52. Others have drawn a connection between the "fiery ordeal" and the Messianic woes; see Mark Dubis, *Messianic Woes in First Peter: Suffering and Eschatology in 1 Peter 4:12–19* (New York: P. Lang, 2002); Bo Reicke, *The Epistles of James, Peter and Jude,* The Anchor Bible (New York: Doubleday, 1964), 71–72; and Ernest Best, *1 Peter*, New Century Bible (Greenwood, S.C.: Attic Press, 1971), 161. To simply see the fiery trial as historical in nature is not sufficient for the full-orbed view of persecution and suffering in the life of a Christian. It is likely

1. *Persecution*. This is likely what Peter has in view. Early Christians lived in the heat of being imprisoned, slandered, maligned, discriminated against, marginalized, and even killed. This kind of persecution has been present since the beginning and still puts Christians in the furnace in many parts of the world (John 15:18; Heb. 11:32–38).

2. *Temptation*. James says, "Blessed is the man that endureth temptation: for when he is tried, he shall receive the crown of life, which the Lord hath promised to them that love him" (James 1:12). Whenever temptations arise, there is an opportunity for the one who is tempted to respond by sinning or triumphing over sin. God never tempts His people in the sense that He would cause their sin, but the devil seeks the downfall of the Lord's people when their hearts are weak and easily drawn away (cf. James 1:14).

3. *Providence*. These are common trials that come in life. They can range from mild to severe, temporary to permanent, obvious to hidden. They are physical, mental, and emotional. They can be brought on by or lead to illness or disability. They include griefs and sorrows. They affect families, workplaces, and churches. They are uncontrolled, as in economic and natural situations. They revolve around spiritual afflictions, such as desertions and perplexing providences. In all these ways, afflictions of God's providence can come at any time and touch any facet of our lives.

These three aspects, either separate or together, are what Peter has in mind when he uses the words "fiery trial."[12] This is how Peter wishes us to think of Christian suffering. It is a fiery trial. It is a refiner's furnace. By giving it such a clear name, Peter has already succeeded in making it less strange, and so "we must see good in that, in which other men can see none."[13]

The Designer
Second, the fiery trial should not seem strange because God has fashioned and designed this furnace. Put a man in a dire situation and tell him an

---

that Peter has in view all undeserved Christian suffering, as he earlier exhorts his readers to set their minds on the hope to be given at the appearing of Christ (see 1 Peter 1:13). Only Christ's coming will finally and fully relieve all Christians from the suffering they experience in this life.

12. Cf. Green, *1 Peter*, 155.

13. John Bunyan, *The Entire Works of John Bunyan*, vol. 2, ed. Henry Stebbing (London: James S. Virtue, 1860), 285.

enemy or stranger has devised it, and he will have reason to think the situation strange. But if the situation comes from the hand of his father, a father who knows his needs and weaknesses, the man need not think such a situation strange. It has been fashioned by his own father. How much more should we be comforted, then, by the knowledge that our afflictions are given to us by the Father of lights (James 1:17)? John Flavel wrote, "It is the great support and solace of the saints in all the distresses that befall them here, that there is a wise Spirit sitting in all the wheels of motion, and governing the most eccentric creatures and their most pernicious designs to blessed and happy issues."[14] What Amos writes about evil in the city also applies to the Christian's affliction: "Shall there be evil in a city, and the LORD hath not done it" (Amos 3:6). In other words: Shall there be a furnace through which we must pass that the Lord Himself has not designed? Thomas Brooks said:

> There is no sickness so little God but hath a finger in it, though it be but the acting of the little finger. And as the scribe is more eyed, and more properly said to write, than the pen; and as every workman is more eyed, and more properly said to effect his work, than the tools which he uses as his instruments: the Lord, who is the chief agent and mover in all actions, and who has the greatest hand in all our afflictions, is far more to be eyed and owned than any inferior or subordinate causes whatever.[15]

Every furnace the Christian endures comes from the sovereign and all-sufficient God: "Whoever brings an affliction, it is God that sends it."[16] Thus, the furnace is ultimately God's and serves for our good (cf. Rom. 8:28).

The Examples
Third, the fiery trial should not seem strange because the Scriptures give us many examples of God's people in the furnace. Israel's suffering in Egypt is pictured as suffering in the furnace. Jehovah says, "Behold, I have

---

14. John Flavel, *The Whole Works of the Rev. Mr. John Flavel*, 6 vols. (London: W. Baynes and Son, 1820), 4:342–43.

15. Thomas Brooks, *The Mute Christian Under the Smarting Rod; With Sovereign Antidotes for Every Case* (London: W. Nicholson, 1806), 26–27.

16. Thomas Watson, *A Body of Practical Divinity in a Series of Sermons on the Shorter Catechism* (Aberdeen: George King, 1838), 661.

refined thee, but not with silver; I have chosen thee in the furnace of affliction" (Isa. 48:10; see also Deut. 4:20; 1 Kings 8:51; Jer. 11:4). As the furnace refines, so the exodus was a refining of God's "peculiar treasure" (see Ex. 19:4–5). A Scottish minister once assured, "Adversity is the diamond dust Heaven polishes its jewels with."[17]

There are stories of God's people in the furnace. Very memorable is the account of Daniel's three friends, Shadrach, Meshach, and Abednego. These three youth were literally thrown into a fiery furnace because of their refusal to bow before the king's idol (Daniel 3). They were thrust into this furnace of affliction to be tested and tried in their faith. Further, in several places throughout the Old Testament, God's people are seen as being in the furnace of affliction. The psalmist, declaring God's praises, wrote, "For thou, O God, hast proved us; thou hast tried us, as silver is tried" (Ps. 66:10). God, speaking of making Himself known, declared through Zechariah, "And I will bring the third part through the fire, and will refine them as silver is refined, and will try them as gold is tried: they shall call on my name, and I will hear them: I will say, It is my people: and they shall say, The LORD is my God" (Zech. 13:9). Again, prophesying of the messianic days, Malachi proclaims, "And he shall sit as a refiner and purifier of silver: and he shall purify the sons of Levi, and purge them as gold and silver, that they may offer unto the LORD an offering in righteousness" (Mal. 3:3).[18]

Each of these passages leaves us to ask: If the saints in former times had the furnace, why should saints today see it a strange thing? Thomas Watson reminded us, "The present state of life is subject to afflictions…. [The Christian] is heir-apparent to it; he comes into the world with a cry, and goes out with a groan."[19] This is the way God has dealt with His people since He first formed and fashioned them in His plan of redemption.

The Remaining Sin
Fourth, the fiery trial should not seem strange because of our sinful natures and remaining sin even after receiving grace. The Bible teaches us that

---

17. Quoted in John Anthony O'Brien, *A Treasury of Great Thoughts from Ancient to Modern Times* (New York: F. Fell Publishers, 1973), 345.
18. Cf. Thomas R. Schreiner, *First, Second Peter, Jude*, New American Commentary (Nashville, Tenn.: B&H, 2003), 219.
19. Watson, *A Body of Practical Divinity*, 661.

God places His people in affliction in order to expose their sin. One thinks of Israel grumbling in the wilderness. God, revealing their sin to them, afflicted them with fiery serpents until the people repented of their sin (Num. 21:4–9). Likewise, David, after committing adultery, was afflicted by the loss of God's presence until he was brought to plead with God to cleanse him of his sin (Ps. 51:2). Both nationally and individually, God was known to afflict His people to bring them to a renewed understanding of the sin that remained in them. Similarly, even the apostle Paul spoke of the thorn in his flesh sent from Satan. Regardless of what this thorn was, it is clear that Paul was afflicted and it is clear that it was an instrument used to reveal to Paul the dangers of pride (2 Cor. 12:6–8).[20] Thomas Manton observed, "Afflictions occasion experience of God and trial of grace, and are a part of God's discipline for the mortifying of sin, happy opportunities to discover more of God to us."[21]

In these times, it is easy for God's people to feel that their sins become more visible and rise to the surface. But the struggle of sin, which begins at the point of conversion, highlights the effectual working of grace in true believers' lives. Afflictions may seem to bring out the worst in us, but they also serve to make us see sin we never saw before—and this is for our good. George Whitefield once noted, "Afflictions don't *bring* the dross; they *reveal* the dross."

Perhaps this is why Christians going through affliction are often misunderstood by those around them. Those of us who are trying to help those who are tried can easily fall into the same trap that Job's friends did. Rather than being quick to accuse them when we see sins and weaknesses coming to the surface during afflictions, we should have sympathy for them, as Job begged his friends to do: "Have pity upon me, have pity upon me, O ye my friends; for the hand of God hath touched me" (Job 19:21). And remember, if you are not in the furnace yourself right now, you may be soon. We should do what Christ did at Lazarus's tomb, as Mary and Martha were going through the furnace of grief: He wept (John 11:35). We should do what Paul says: "Weep with them that weep" (Rom 12:15).

---

20. See John Calvin, *Commentary on the Epistles of Paul the Apostle to the Corinthians*, trans. John Pringle, vol. 1 (reprint, Grand Rapids: Eerdmans, 2009), 371–77.

21. Thomas Manton, *One Hundred and Ninety Sermons on the Hundred and Nineteenth Psalm*, vol. 3 (London: William Brown, 1845), 329.

Let's pray for compassionate and humble hearts toward our suffering brothers and sisters, and remember that in light of remaining sin, suffering should not seem strange. After all, through afflictions, God is refining us, bringing our sins to the surface in order to skim them off. Christians ought not to find afflictions strange because "there is more evil in a drop of sin than in a sea of affliction."[22]

The Suffering Life

Fifth, the fiery trial should not seem strange because the Christian life is defined as one of costly suffering. Christ did not sell the Christian life as one of ease, comfort, and prosperity. This is not the promise of the covenant of grace. Rather, quite the opposite: "Whosoever will come after me, let him deny himself, and take up his cross, and follow me. For whosoever will save his life shall lose it; but whosoever shall lose his life for my sake and the gospel's, the same shall save it" (Mark 8:34–35). Jesus even commands His disciples to embrace a life of cross-centered affliction. Manton once preached: "We must every day be ready. As porters stand in the street waiting for a burden for them to carry if they be hired to it, so must a Christian every day be prepared to take up his burden, if God shall call him to it."[23] And Whitefield journaled: "Whilst I continue on this side of eternity, I never expect to be free from trials, only to change them. For it is necessary to heal the pride of my heart that such should come."[24]

Paul summarizes Christ's teaching as follows: "We must through much tribulation enter into the kingdom of God" (Acts 14:22). And he even *desires* "the fellowship of [Christ's] sufferings" (Phil. 3:10). The Christian life is one of suffering and partaking of Christ's suffering: "Inasmuch as you are partakers of Christ's sufferings" (1 Peter 2:13). While these are not meritorious sufferings, they are a means of sanctifying us and conforming us *to Christ*. As Nathanael Vincent once stated, "A rare sight it is indeed to see a man coming out of a bed of languishing, or any other furnace of affliction, more like to angels in purity, more like to Christ who was holy, harmless, undefiled, and separate from sinners; more like unto God Himself, being

---

22. Watson, *A Body of Practical Divinity*, 131.
23. Manton, *Sermons*, 329.
24. George Whitefield, *George Whitefield's Journals* (Edinburgh: Banner of Truth, 1998), 179.

more exactly righteous in all his ways and more exemplarily holy in all manner of conversation."[25] The furnace of affliction is the very definition of a Christlike life; should we expect anything different?

The Character of God

Sixth, the fiery trial should not seem strange because to complain against suffering is to rebel against God and His character. When we look at affliction as a strange thing, as something that should not be happening, we have the occasion to rebel against the will of God for our life (cf. Rom. 8:28). We can often be led to question the character of God. The Israelites complained about the difficulties in the wilderness by accusing God of bringing them into the wilderness to kill them, but their redemption was the reason for their affliction. Calling God's character into question led to unbelief and faithless thoughts regarding God, His purposes, and His love. Times of trial should not be times of unbelief. "Let us make a right judgment of afflictions," wrote Stephen Charnock. "The flesh makes us think God often to be our enemy when He is our friend."[26] Times of affliction should be times when we trust in the righteousness, goodness, and kindness of our Father.

Unbelief can breed in us a tendency to grumble and murmur because we think too highly of ourselves and what we deserve. This is what we see in Job and Asaph. Job, when he was afflicted, was at first patient. But over time, Job began to consider the suffering "strange." Moved by the instigation of his friends' accusations and through the weakness of his own mind, Job began to question God, going so far as to curse the day of his own birth (see Job 3:1). But Job's afflictions were given to him to show him how weak and insignificant he was and how great God was. When he realized this, Job laid his hand on his mouth and stopped murmuring against God (Job 40:4).

Likewise, Asaph, looking at his own circumstances and the prosperity of the world, was led to think he deserved to be prosperous and happy. In his affliction, he grumbled: "I was envious at the foolish" (Ps. 73:3). We often find the trials that come our way strange if

---

25. Quoted in Charles Spurgeon, *The Treasury of David*, vol. 6 (New York: Funk and Wagnalls, 1882), 176.

26. Stephen Charnock, *The Works of Stephen Charnock*, vol. 3 (London: Paternoster Row, 1816), 297.

we are nurturing ingratitude for the blessings God has given us or if we are comparing present circumstances between ourselves and others. Grumbling is a failure to see how rich we are, how undeserved our mercies are, how free God's gifts are. Joseph Hall showed the spirit we ought to have when we experience the furnace of affliction: "O God, if Thy bellows did not sometimes thus breathe upon me in spiritual repercussions, I should have just cause to suspect my estate. Those few weak gleeds of grace that are in me might soon go out if they were not thus refused. Still blow upon them till they kindle, still kindle them till they flame up to Thee."[27] As Asaph later testified, "Thou shalt...receive me to glory" (Ps. 73:24). How important it is to fight worldly thinking about life and about what we think we deserve.

The Presence of God

Seventh, the fiery trial should not seem strange because God is with His people in it. God's presence with His people in their suffering was promised in Isaiah: "When thou passest through the waters, I will be with thee; and through the rivers, they shall not overflow thee: when thou walkest through the fire, thou shalt not be burned; neither shall the flame kindle upon thee" (43:2). He further prophesied of God's being with His people: "In all their affliction he was afflicted, and the angel of his presence saved them: in his love and in his pity he redeemed them; and he bare them, and carried them all the days of old" (Isa. 63:9).

This is clearly illustrated in the story of Daniel's three friends. The fiery furnace into which King Nebuchadnezzar threw Shadrach, Meshach, and Abednego had an opening, through which the king looked in to see how quickly these men would burn to ashes. What he saw astonished him: "Did not we cast three men bound into the midst of the fire? They answered and said unto the king, True, O king. Look! He answered and said, Lo, I see four men loose, walking in the midst of the fire, and they have no hurt; and the form of the fourth is like the Son of God" (Dan. 3:24–25). This was none other than Christ, Immanuel—"God with us"—in the furnace with them: "Can you so trust in the living God as to feel sure that when you get into the midst

---

27. Joseph Hall, "Occasional Mediations," XXII, in *The Works of the Right Reverend Joseph Hall*, ed. Philip Wynter (Oxford: Oxford University Press, 1863), 10:131.

of the burning fiery furnace, there will be with you one like unto the Son of God, who will preserve you by his gracious presence?"[28]

It is often in afflictions that God's people have the greatest sense of God's intimate presence. They can say with Paul, "All men forsook me...[but] the Lord stood with me" (2 Tim. 4:16–17). Sometimes God walks closest to us through our afflictions.

Thus, should the fiery trial be strange to us, when He who is our Lord and Savior, our Master and Friend, is there with us in the midst of our affliction? "If God be for us, who can be against us?... Who shall separate us from the love of Christ? shall tribulation, or distress, or persecution, or famine, or nakedness, or peril, or sword?... For I am persuaded, that neither death, nor life, nor angels, nor principalities, nor powers, nor things present, nor things to come, nor height, nor depth, nor any other creature, shall be able to separate us from the love of God, which is in Christ Jesus our Lord" (Rom. 8:31, 35, 38–39).

In all our suffering, God is watching over us, as John Downame once said, "The Lord does not only behold our tribulation as it were afar off, He being included in heaven, as we are in the earth...as the careful physician watches over his patient...so the Lord stands by us, that when we are according to His own mind purged and purified."[29]

But God does not simply relate with His people in their suffering, He further *enters into our afflictions*—namely, by sending Christ to suffer and die. As Samuel Rutherford consoled, "Ye know that the weightiest end of the cross of Christ that is laid upon you lieth upon your strong Saviour."[30] We also remember that when Christ appeared to Paul on the road to Damascus, He questioned, "Saul, Saul, why persecutest thou me?" (Acts 9:4). The sufferings of Christ's people are the afflictions of Christ Himself (cf. Col. 1:24), who is with us in all our furnaces. He went through the fires of Gethsemane and Golgotha to pay for the sins of His people, so they would not need to. He had to go through the flame of God's wrath so that the fires of God's wrath would be extinguished for His people, and "if God be

---

28. C. H. Spurgeon, *The Metropolitan Tabernacle* (London: Passmore and Alabaster, 1904), 161.

29. John Downame, cited in R. A. Bertram, *A Homiletic Encyclopedia* (New York: Funk & Wagnalls, 1885), 31.

30. Samuel Rutherford, *Letters of Samuel Rutherford* (Edinburgh: Banner of Truth, 2006), 34.

with us, if the power of Christ will rest upon us, then we may even 'glory in infirmities.'"[31]

The Freedom

Eighth, the fiery trial should not seem strange because of the freedom that it brings. Daniel's three friends not only experienced Christ's presence in the midst of the furnace, but not a hair on their heads was singed because of Him, and no smell of fire was on their clothes (Dan. 3:27). But we are told something else amazing. There was one thing that the fire did burn. It burned the cords that bound them. Before they entered the fire, they were bound and could not walk, but the fire, the source of their affliction, enabled them to walk freely.

There is a spiritual parallel here. It is the constant testimony of the Lord's people who go through the fires of persecution or adversity that the Lord not only protects them from the fire, but He uses the fire to burn the things that still bind them: "So we before did not know that there were such unmortified lusts in the soul, till the storm of affliction comes, then we spy unbelief, impatience, carnal fear, we see it drop down in many places."[32]

Perhaps it is the fear of man from which we are freed. Perhaps we are freed from a love for this world. Perhaps we are freed from a fear of death. God uses affliction, troubles, and persecution to give His people liberty. Martin Luther experienced this freedom at the Diet of Worms, when he fearlessly defied the papal courts. This was the common experience of the Scottish missionary John Paton, who knew serious afflictions firsthand but was continually freed from discouragement, distress, and danger while working among the cannibals on the island of Tanna. As Richard Sibbes commented, "Poverty and affliction take away the fuel that feeds pride."[33] And this is the testimony of Paul, who, though facing death, was freed from self-reliance by the God who raises the dead (cf. 2 Cor. 1:8–11).

Should, then, the fiery trial seem strange to believers if it serves to free them from those things that bind them? Often Christ leads us

---

31. Thomas Manton, *The Complete Works of Thomas Manton*, vol. 7 (London: James Nisbet & Co., 1872), 31.

32. Watson, *A Body of Practical Divinity*, 664.

33. Richard Sibbes, *The Works of Richard Sibbes*, vol. 6 (Edinburgh: James Nichol, 1863), 239.

through the furnace of affliction so we can experience the freedom He marvelously works for us.

The Lord's Designs and Desires

Ninth, the fiery trial should not seem strange because its end results are entirely in line with God's designs and desires for His people. This is exactly what Peter means when he explains: "That the trial of your faith, being much more precious than of gold that perisheth, though it be tried with fire, might be found unto praise and honour and glory at the appearing of Jesus Christ" (1 Peter 1:7).

We might be tempted to shrink from the suffering, but the furnace does not hurt the gold and silver put in it. Brooks wrote, "The design of God in all the afflictions that befall [His people] is only to try them; it is not to wrong nor ruin them, as ignorant men are apt to think."[34]

The furnace only makes the gold and silver purer metals. God's people are called His special treasure, His gold and silver. At times, nothing less than a fiery trial is needed to purify such a precious people. The afflicted heart is "a gracious heart [which] cleaves nearer and nearer to God in affliction, and can justify God in his severe strokes, acknowledging them to be all just and holy."[35] Just as a plow suggests the potential usefulness of the ground and the pruning knife suggests the fruitfulness of a tree, even more the furnace implies the preciousness of the people of God. Downame wrote: "When the oil of spiritual grace will not mollify our iron hearts, then God makes them soft in the fiery furnace of tribulation. When they are such stiff grounds...He breaks up, ploughs, and harrows them with afflictions, that so they may become fruitful."[36] And Rutherford urged, "I am persuaded your Physician will not slay you, but purge you, seeing He calleth Himself the Surgeon, who maketh the wound and bindeth it up again; for to lance a wound is not to kill but to cure the patient."[37] Should we then think it strange?

---

34. Thomas Brooks, *Precious Remedies Against Satan's Devices: Being, A Companion For Christians of All Denominations* (Philadelphia: Jonathan Pounder, 1810), 94.

35. Flavel, *The Works*, 5:620.

36. Downame, cited in Bertram, *Homiletic Encyclopedia*, 10.

37. Rutherford, *Letters*, 97.

The Joy

Tenth, the fiery trial should not seem strange because, if it does, it robs us of our joy. First Peter 4:13 shows that the opposite of thinking such fiery trials strange is a command to rejoice: "But rejoice" (cf. Matt. 5:11–12). Bishop Leighton put it well: "If the children of God consider their trials, not in their natural bitterness, but in the sweet love whence they spring, and the sweet fruits that spring from them, that we are our Lord's gold, and that he tries us in the furnace to purify us…this may beget not only patience, but gladness even in the sufferings."[38]

Afflictions conform God's precious people to Christ, their Head. This conformity is the cause of joy unspeakable and full of glory. Through faith, suffering believers can sing, "Behind a frowning providence, He hides a smiling face."[39] Rutherford gives a glimpse of such an unspeakable joy: "Howbeit you receive indignities for your Lord's sake, let it be so. When He shall put His holy hand up to your face, and wipe the tears from your eyes, judge if ye will not have cause then to rejoice."[40]

There is joy in suffering because there is joy in being conformed to God's image (1 Thess. 4:3). We ought not to think this fiery trial strange, but rather, to desire that the furnace will accomplish God's intended design. Even if we don't understand why God is afflicting us, we should resign ourselves to our afflictions as quickly as possible and approve of God's way of dealing with us. Edward Payson, a godly Puritan minister who was often greatly tried, was asked if he could see any particular reason for the heavy trials with which he was afflicted. He replied: "No, but I am as well satisfied as if I could see ten thousand. God's will is the very perfection of all reasons."[41]

Therefore, when facing the furnace of affliction, we should ask ourselves questions such as: "Am I walking by faith and fighting worldliness? Am I devoted to God in all areas of life? Am I seeking His presence and favor through the means of grace? Am I sitting loose from the things of this world, and am I ready to depart at whatever time God sees fit for me?" In this way, we will be more ready to

---

38. Robert Leighton, *The Whole Works of Robert Leighton* (New York: J. C. Riker, 1846), 316.

39. From the hymn "God Moves in a Mysterious Way" by William Cowper, 1774.

40. Rutherford, *Letters*, 61.

41. Cited in Asa Cummings, *A Memoir of the Rev. Edward Payson* (Boston: Crocker and Brewster, 1830), 353.

benefit from trials that the Lord lays upon us: "God's stretching the strings of His viol, is to make the music better."[42]

Conclusion

This chapter has briefly considered ten reasons why we ought not to think God's fiery furnace strange. This is absurdly different from much of theology that is rampant today, such as the so-called health-and-wealth gospel. It would have many believe that Christians will always live prosperous lives if they only have enough faith. And countless numbers are being led to believe that suffering should be a "strange" experience. This goes against everything the Scriptures proclaim! And it contrasts with the solid theology of the Puritans. We are not to think it strange.

A final question to address is how Peter could write the things he did about affliction. Perhaps Peter would say something like this to us: "There was a time when I knew little about this furnace. My Lord kept talking about what He was going to face, about the fact that He would suffer and die, and that we needed to be willing to die as well, but I was not willing to do that. It seemed such a strange idea to me that I 'began to rebuke him' (Mark 8:32). 'This shall not be,' I said (Matt. 16:22). But things came about exactly as my Lord had said. One night, I actually stood near a literal fire, just outside the hall of Caiaphas, and I was asked whether I knew Jesus. There was the fiery trial I had thought so strange. I was right in the middle of it! Three times I was asked whether I knew my Master, and I denied I knew Him three times, even with cursings and an oath. This was a fiery trial for me, and I fell deeply. It revealed so much of my sinful heart. But I came to realize over the days that followed that He was being my Refiner—refining my faith and my life, and skimming off the dross. Later, by the Sea of Tiberias, He asked me: 'Simon, son of Jonas, lovest thou me?' (John 21:17). He was wanting to see His own reflection in me. He had used even my fiery trial to teach me more of myself and of Himself. And He taught me that, in the end, even my death would glorify Him (John 21:19)."

This is not to say that we ought to rush headlong into the furnace. But as we pray to grow in grace and in assurance, we may well find that the Lord will accomplish His purpose for us through the

---

42. Watson, *A Body of Practical Divinity*, 303.

furnace of affliction. And so we must prepare for it, that we do not think it strange.

It is said that Charles and Susannah Spurgeon had a plaque on their bedroom wall with the words of Isaiah 48:10: "I have chosen thee in the furnace of affliction." What a reminder that trials are not strange: "He that rides to be crowned, will not think much of a rainy day."[43] Be encouraged that He who perfectly ordains your trials, and uses them to purify you and to impress more of His own image upon you, will be your shield and strength, and will keep you until the furnace will be forever past, and the righteous shall shine as brilliantly as the sun and stars, to His praise forevermore.

---

43. John Trapp, *Commentary of the Old and New Testaments*, vol. 1 (Eureka, Calif.: Tanski, 1997), 92.

CHAPTER 9

Living Morally in a Sexually Immoral World

Brian Croft

Proverbs 5

Recently I spent some time with a good friend I have known most of my life. He began to tell me he had recently fallen into some really serious sin. I assumed he was going to tell me he had fallen back into pornography, a continuous struggle for him since I have known him. I was not prepared for what he told me. He explained how his struggle with pornography had led him to solicit prostitutes regularly for several months. What caused him to end his steady habit? His wife caught him. As you can imagine, his marriage is in shambles. By the grace of God, his wife has actually stayed with him, and they are being cared for by their church as they put the pieces back together—if they can.

Adultery is perhaps the most painful betrayal that one can experience in this life. It is an epidemic in our country and, sadly, the church as well. For this reason, the wisdom God offers from the book of Proverbs on this matter serves us well in protecting each of us from this kind of destructive unfaithfulness.

The proverbs were written by Solomon for his son so that he would gain wisdom, discernment, insight, and understanding as to how to live in God's world in a way that shows a fear of the Lord. The proverbs are not to be taken as promises; they are general truths that provide the wisdom and discernment needed to live rightly in this world filled with sin.

In Proverbs 5, God gives wisdom about how to be a faithful husband and how to protect oneself from the allurements of the adulterous woman. This chapter presents God's design for marriage and physical intimacy, and shows how we are to deal with the greatest enemy of that design in the midst of the constant bombardment of sexual immorality in our culture. These are important matters whether you are a husband or wife, single or married, widowed or divorced, old or young:

> My son, attend unto my wisdom, and bow thine ear to my understanding: that thou mayest regard discretion, and that thy lips may keep knowledge. For the lips of a strange woman drop as an honeycomb, and her mouth is smoother than oil: but her end is bitter as wormwood, sharp as a twoedged sword. Her feet go down to death; her steps take hold on hell. Lest thou shouldest ponder the path of life, her ways are moveable, that thou canst not know them. Hear me now therefore, O ye children, and depart not from the words of my mouth. Remove thy way far from her, and come not nigh the door of her house: lest thou give thine honour unto others, and thy years unto the cruel: lest strangers be filled with thy wealth; and thy labours be in the house of a stranger; and thou mourn at the last, when thy flesh and thy body are consumed, and say, How have I hated instruction, and my heart despised reproof; and have not obeyed the voice of my teachers, nor inclined mine ear to them that instructed me! I was almost in all evil in the midst of the congregation and assembly. Drink waters out of thine own cistern, and running waters out of thine own well. Let thy fountains be dispersed abroad, and rivers of waters in the streets. Let them be only thine own, and not strangers' with thee. Let thy fountain be blessed: and rejoice with the wife of thy youth. Let her be as the loving hind and pleasant roe; let her breasts satisfy thee at all times; and be thou ravished always with her love. And why wilt thou, my son, be ravished with a strange woman, and embrace the bosom of a stranger? For the ways of man are before the eyes of the LORD, and he pondereth all his goings. His own iniquities shall take the wicked himself, and he shall be holden with the cords of his sins. He shall die without instruction; and in the greatness of his folly he shall go astray.

In this chapter, God reveals three instructions to husbands about His good design for marriage.

Flee the Adulterous Woman

First, husbands should flee from the adulterous woman (vv. 1–14). The adulterous woman, referenced all throughout Proverbs, is a woman who tries to lure men away from their wives and to her. Solomon warns his son about the cunning efforts of the adulterous woman: "Remove thy way far from her, and come not nigh the door of her house" (v. 8).

In Genesis 2, God tells us His good and perfect purpose for the man and woman He created in His image. They were one flesh, naked and not ashamed (vv. 24–25). Marriage is a divine design from our good God between one man and one woman for life. However, ever since the fall of man, recorded in Genesis 3, God's design for man and woman as a one-flesh union has been distorted in all sorts of ways, something that continues in our culture today with homosexuality, pornography, and sexual abuse. Perhaps even more insidious is the glamorization of infidelity in television and movies, a perversion that no longer disturbs many of us, as evidenced by the fact that so many within the church watch it. The adulterous woman of Proverbs represents these corruptions of God's good and perfect design for marriage.

Solomon lists two reasons we must flee from her. First, the adulterous woman disguises her destruction with beauty (vv. 1–6). This is why the devil is often described as a beautiful woman in a red dress. The adulterous woman is good at luring men into her clutches because her lips "drop as an honeycomb, and her mouth is smoother than oil" (v. 3). She appeals to men by making them think that she will offer them what they want and what will satisfy them. However, as so many men have discovered after drinking her seduction, she uses her beauty and her crafty words to hide her destruction: "But her end is bitter as wormwood, sharp as a twoedged sword. Her feet go down to death; her steps take hold on hell. Lest thou shouldest ponder the path of life, her ways are moveable, that thou canst not know them" (vv. 4–6).

She is a wolf in sheep's clothing. Though she disguises herself with beauty and smooth words (v. 3), those who are lured by her learn that she leads only to destruction.

Second, we must flee the adulterous woman because embracing her assures disastrous consequences (vv. 7–14). Solomon reminds his son to "remove thy way far from her, and come not nigh the door of her house" (v. 8). Notice the long list of horrible consequences if we do not heed these words:

> Lest thou give thine honour unto others, and thy years unto the cruel: lest strangers be filled with thy wealth; and thy labours be in the house of a stranger; and thou mourn at the last, when thy flesh and thy body are consumed, and say, How have I hated instruction, and my heart despised reproof; and have not obeyed the voice of my teachers, nor inclined mine ear to them that instructed me! (vv. 9–13)

What a despairing place to be—when you yield yourself to the adulterous woman, reap these consequences, and only then realize, "I have not obeyed the voice of my teachers, nor inclined mine ear to them that instructed me" (v. 13).

Anyone who has encountered the lure of an adulterous woman realizes how chillingly accurate this description in Proverbs actually is. I was confronted with a woman like this through some ministry situations. This woman was very attractive and her speech was smoother than oil (v. 3). Yet the destruction listed by Solomon was evidenced in her four failed marriages, rampant drug abuse, and dysfunctional personal relationships. My wife was very aware of the moments when I had to deal with this woman, but the most memorable time was when Pastor Scott Wells happened to be with me and saw the way this woman acted toward me. Once we left, before I even had a chance to bring it up, he said to me in his subtle, military, Alabama boy manner, "I don't care what you do, you stay as far from that woman as humanly possible." It was good advice, and I have heeded it.

Whether it is that woman at work who is a bit flirtatious with you, that neighbor who seems to walk across the street to talk with you a bit too much, or that employee at the bank or store who takes a little too much interest in your personal life, heed the words of Pastor Wells and, more importantly, Solomon: "Remove thy way far from her, and come not nigh the door of her house" (v. 8). Remember, the adulterous woman lures you in with her flirtatious speech and flattery. Do not be lulled into thinking it is no big deal when you find yourself enjoying her attention. Give attention to wisdom, incline your ear to understanding, observe discretion, and do not be deceived by the empty words of the adulterous woman.

In all likelihood, most committed Christians do not enter into affairs with the adulterous woman. Far more, however, sin sexually with the virtual adulterous woman, the adulterous woman found in pornography. Any pursuit of pornography is a pursuit of the adulterous woman herself. Just like the flesh-and-blood adulteress, the digital adulteress will steal your affections from God and your wife. Pornography is an epidemic, not just in this country, but in the church. It is such a big problem because it does what is described here. It lures men (and women, for that matter) with its smooth promises. Yet all find out that, just like the adulterous woman, its "end is bitter as wormwood" (v. 4).

If you are struggling with pornography in any way, you are teasing the adulterous woman. For those who think it is no big deal, tell that to my friend I mentioned earlier, the one whose tailspin into gross sexual immorality started with "just pornography." That's not to mention a figure like Ted Bundy, who traced his heinous crimes against women back to one exposure to pornography. Dear brothers and sisters, married or single, if you are being tempted by the sexually explicit material all around us, *keep your way far from it*. This may mean some drastic accountability with regard to Internet use and even the more subtle television shows you watch. Regardless, we are to flee from the adulterous woman because God has a different and better design and plan for us.

Delight in Your Wife

The second instruction God gives about His good design for marriage is for husbands to delight solely in their wives (vv. 15–20). One of the most profound truths that I was taught and that has consistently benefitted my own marriage and all the marriage counseling that I do is this: a wife is a husband's greatest protection from the adulterous woman and the allurements of sexual sin surrounding us. We find the reason why this is true as Solomon turns his thoughts from the adulterous woman and shows his son how and why he should solely delight in his wife.

Solomon gives three reasons for this. The first is because she is yours (vv. 15–17). Notice the language Solomon uses here to describe how husbands and wives belong to each other, revealing the beautiful "one-flesh" union: "Drink waters out of thine own cistern, and running waters out of thine own well. Let thy fountains be dispersed abroad, and rivers of waters in the streets. Let them be only thine own, and not strangers' with thee."

God has given your wife to you exclusively, to have and enjoy. But God has also given you the responsibility to protect her from others who would try to enjoy her in the same way: "let them be only thine own, and not strangers' with thee" (v. 17). God's design for marriage is that all our physical affections, desires, and enjoyment be directed exclusively to our spouses.

The second reason a man should delight exclusively in his wife is because she is satisfying (vv. 18–19). There is little need to explain verses 18 and 19. It is obvious that any sexual desires a man has are to be directed entirely toward his wife, and her alone. Notice the words used to describe how a husband should feel toward his wife: he is to *rejoice* in, be *satisfied* by, and be *ravished* by the love of his wife. Husbands, does this describe you and your feelings toward your wives? This is God's design; anything that would steal these desires from a man's heart for his wife is a perversion of God's good plan.

The third reason a man should delight exclusively in his wife is because she is your protection: "Why wilt thou, my son, be ravished with a strange woman, and embrace the bosom of a stranger?" (v. 20). The fact that the wife is the husband's protection has shown itself true in my own marriage and in the marriage counseling I do. In other words, why would you pursue the adulterous woman when you have this wife whom God has given you to enjoy, delight in, and be captivated by—especially given all the consequences for doing so?

God's design is truly amazing. He calls both husbands and wives to protect the other from the greatest dangers of this world. Men are to protect their wives from physical harm, which is why Peter says a man must realize his wife is the weaker vessel (1 Peter 3:7). Likewise, wives play just as important a role in being the chief protection provided by God for their husbands from the adulterous woman. Husbands, delight in your wives, for they are your protection from the snare of this woman. Wives, see and embrace this significant role you play in caring for and protecting your husbands from this woman.

God's design is clear. Why, then, do we so often fight against it? One major implication of Solomon's words is that God has given all we need in our wives to be captivated by their love. I am not talking only about physical intimacy, but the whole person of our wives. If this does not describe you today, you need to ask yourself this important question: "Why am I not rejoicing in my wife as I should?" When we cannot answer that question as we should, we are quick to point the finger at our wives and say it is something they are doing. The reality, however, is that we have grown to take our wives for granted. We have forgotten what caused us to be so captivated by their love that we vowed to spend our lives with them.

Be reminded that this passage expresses how we should feel toward our wives, something Paul says is ultimately seen as we love our wives "even as Christ also loved the church, and gave himself for it" (Eph. 5:25). We are to experience life with our wives in this way, not just because it is God's design for us to be satisfied in our lifelong companions, but more importantly, it is how the gospel is displayed to the world that is watching whether we love, adore, cherish, and are captivated by every aspect of our wives.

A helpful question I have been asked in regard to this passage is this: "So, how will you apply this passage to women?" Though I am not a woman, by God's kind providence I am married to a good one. And she has loved me enough to teach me that there are legitimate reasons why a woman's desire for physical intimacy ebbs and flows through different seasons of life. Those married for several years and those who have had children require no explanation. Husbands, be very aware that this is true across the board, including *your* wives, and be sensitive and understanding to your wives as they communicate this reality to you.

Three encouragements for wives come out of this passage. First, every woman must guard herself from becoming the adulterous woman. There is never an acceptable circumstance where a woman can and should pursue another woman's husband. It is a complete perversion of God's design. If that describes you, do not ignore the heinousness of the adulterous woman's sin. Yet, if you are the adulterous woman, you are not beyond the mercy of God in Christ. There can be forgiveness for you, but you must repent and flee to Christ, realizing that only in Him can there be cleansing from this sin.

Second, beware of the adulterous woman. She is out there, and I dare say she is the greatest asset to the enemy. Know she is out there to steal your husband, and you are his greatest protection from her. Do not close yourself off from your husband because you are mad at him, want something from him, or want to send him some hidden message. In doing so, you are removing a major protection from your husband's fight against this woman.

Third, see God's beautiful, good, and perfect design for physical intimacy for you in this passage. Solomon is not at all saying this is to be a one-sided deal. You should experience the same delight with your husband as he should experience with you. There are many obstacles in a woman's life to this: a selfish and insensitive husband, children, stress, physical struggles that work against this, and others. Envision God's good plan for you. Pray that you would experience what God has intended, regardless of the obstacles that may work against it.

Tremble before God

The third and final instruction God gives about His good design for marriage is that we should tremble before our omniscient God (vv. 21–23). This million-dollar word *omniscient* simply means that God knows all things. There is nothing hidden from His sight (Heb. 4:13). It is not a coincidence that Solomon warns about the adulterous woman, shows God's true design for us in marriage, and then reminds us that the God of the universe knows and sees all things. Sexual sins are the sins we are most tempted to try to hide. Yet nothing can be hidden from our omniscient God.

Solomon provides important reasons why we must tremble before Him. The first is because God knows our ways. Solomon affirms this, saying, "for the ways of man are before the eyes of the LORD, and he pondereth all his goings" (v. 21). God knows if you have been a faithful husband and He knows if you have not.

The second reason we must tremble before our all-knowing God is because God knows our depravity. This depravity is described as the propensity to be "holden with the cords of his sin" (v. 22). Solomon explains why in verse 23: "in the greatness of his folly, he shall go astray." God knows that because we are born sinners and rebels against Him, we are that much more wired to desire the adulterous woman and to ignore the beautiful design of marriage that God has for us. God knows it is the problem of sin in our hearts that causes the pursuit of these perversions to His plan.

Dear brothers, if you have indulged the temptation of the adulterous woman or the perversions she represents, God knows. You may have successfully kept it from everyone in your life, but God knows. Dear sisters, if you are the adulterous woman or you have sinned against your husbands by closing yourself off from them for selfish gain, God knows. All these sins, as well as all the others, are deserving of God's righteous wrath and judgment. What are we to do if we find ourselves in this place?

There is no sexual sin so heinous that it is beyond the mercy of God experienced in the saving work of Jesus Christ. For Jesus lived the perfect life we could not, then went to the cross as the perfect sacrifice for our sins and died in our place. Jesus paid the debt for not just our sins against God's design for marriage, but for all our sins—once for all. Jesus was also raised three days later, providing forgiveness from sin and eternal life to anyone who would turn from sins and by faith trust in Christ.

Christian friends, you know this gospel and have experienced freedom from sin and joy in being reconciled to God through Christ. We deal with the kinds of sins this passage warns about in the same way we deal with all sin—we confess the sin to God, knowing that He knows it all; repent; turn from it; and run to the arms of our Savior and King, knowing our salvation is not because of anything we have done, but because of what Christ has accomplished on our behalf on the cross. Our forgiveness is because of Him. Our righteousness is through Him. A faithful husband or a faithful wife is not one who always does everything right, but one who is quick to acknowledge sin, repent of it, and walk in the joy of forgiveness in the gospel. Are you that faithful husband? Are you that faithful wife?

By God's grace, may both husbands and wives embrace this design God has for us. May we protect each other in it. May we delight in one another because of it. May the gospel shine forth in the way we love, cherish, and give our whole self to the other just as Christ gave His own life for us. By God's grace, we, as transformed followers of the Lord Jesus Christ, can live in this sexually immoral world in such a way that displays Christ and the glory of our great God.

CHAPTER 10

Living Positively in a Negative Culture

David Murray

Philippians 4:8

We live in an increasingly negative culture, one in which it's easy to be dragged down by all the discouraging and depressing events that flood our hearts and overwhelm our minds.

The recession, foreclosures, unemployment, and family breakdown dominate our media. The cost of college, health care, and senior care is soaring as job openings, house values, savings, and pension funds are shrinking.

The church is increasingly marginalized as politicians, judges, journalists, and educators combine to ridicule fundamental doctrines, to challenge basic Christian morality, and to undermine ancient divine institutions such as marriage.

The Internet and TV bring every tragedy from all corners of the world onto our desktops and into our living rooms every day, feeding us a gloomy and bitter diet of disease, disaster, destruction, and death.

As Christians find themselves increasingly on the losing side of the culture wars, sermons and prayers sound more like discontented defeatism rather than inspirational calls to worship and serve. Our culture seems to be in an unstoppable death spiral, and our moods, mind-sets, and relationships are being dragged down with it.

However, the apostle Paul calls us to an alternative brain diet:

> Finally, brethren, whatsoever things are true, whatsoever things are honest, whatsoever things are just, whatsoever things are pure, whatsoever things are lovely, whatsoever things are of good report; if there be any virtue, and if there be any praise, think on these things. (Phil. 4:8)

In this "Epistle of Joy," Paul is not arguing for unrealistic isolation from the bad news that inevitably fills a fallen world. No, this is not a warrant for monasteries and convents. But it is a warrant, and even a demand, that we choose *a deliberate imbalance* in favor of what is inspirational and wholesome instead of the current imbalance on the side of what is dispiriting and gross.

Garbage In, Garbage Out

This choice will change not only the way we think, but also the way we feel, speak, and act. That's hardly surprising. Just as the quality of the food we put in our mouths affects our thinking, feeling, and doing, so the kinds of words, sounds, and images we put in our ears and eyes has the same effect. Garbage in, garbage out, as they say.

Like us, the Philippian believers were habitual worriers (4:6–7), their minds always racing from one unresolved anxiety to the next. But Paul holds out the prospect of an unimaginable and unsurpassable divine peace to garrison our hearts and minds, a peace that patrols the entrances to our emotions and thoughts. But the way to enjoy that peace patrol is to change what we feed our minds (v. 8).

In other words, if we let what is false, offensive, dishonest, filthy, ugly, and loathsome into our minds, we might as well sign up for a course on how to be hyper-anxious. These interlopers drive peace from the castle, lower the drawbridge, and invite the armies of worry and instability into our mental citadel.

Good In, Good Out

On the other hand, if we starve ourselves of that junk and replace it with what is true, admirable, right, pure, beautiful, and attractive, peace will stand as a sentinel all around our feelings and thoughts, creating an impregnable fortress of calm and tranquility. The peace of God and the God of peace will be with us (vv. 7, 9).

But this takes huge mental effort. "Think on these things," commands Paul. That's not some kind of airy-fairy, freewheeling, blue-sky thinking. It means, "Concentrate and focus on these subjects; form rigorous thinking habits along these lines."

How, then, can we marshal our thoughts into a powerful peace-making and peacekeeping force? Paul lists six areas of a healthy thought life, six categories of thinking, covering many subjects. Let's look at these in turn, especially as they apply to our media diet and then to our ministry diet.

Media Diet

The apostle Paul helps us swim against the powerful riptide by teaching us six strokes. Unless we learn them and use them, we will be easily swept away by the currents of negativity into the whirlpools of fear, anxiety, hate, and depression.

True, Not False

"Whatsoever things are true." Avoid listening to lies, misrepresentation, imbalance, and distortion, on both the left and the right of the political spectrum. Beware of journalists who spend most of their time exposing the lies of "the other team." An overemphasis on falsehood only breeds destructive cynicism, suspicion, mistrust, and hostility.

Instead, seek out the most truthful, balanced, and fair reporting. Read histories and biographies that are accurate rather than sensationalist. Feast on truth wherever it appears and whoever speaks it. Surround yourself with truth-tellers rather than muck-spreaders.

Noble, Not Base

The media tend to publicize the vile and sordid side of life. Their reporters and resources are focused on the seedy cesspools of our society. Instead of reporting and publicizing functioning families and thriving schools, they tend to use their pages and pixels to spotlight failure, brokenness, and disaster.

Have a look over last year's *New York Times* best sellers list. Some of the most popular books were childhood memoirs that described the most horrific abuse and cruelty. One of the best-selling novels celebrated sadistic sex, drawing massive media attention and debasing old and young minds alike.

"Don't do this to yourself!" appeals Paul. Think on "whatsoever things are honest." The word translated as "honest" there means "majestic, awe-inspiring, worthy, and elevating." Its opposite is what is cheap, tawdry, and frivolous. So seek out and consume books, magazines, Web sites, TV programs, movies, and art that elevate the heroic, that inspire awe, and that generate worship. Trash the base and nourish the noble in your life.

Right, Not Wrong

"Whatsoever things are just." When Paul says we should think about the "just," he means that which conforms to God's law and standards; in other words, right conduct in all of life. Does that sound like most sitcoms, soap operas, and news features? Do the media celebrate right acts? Quite the reverse; they focus on sinful acts. People striving to live righteous lives do not make news headlines, and if they are ever pictured in TV or on film, they are usually caricatured as out of touch, pitiable, contemptible, or irrelevant.

Paul urges us to seek out and celebrate right behavior, courageous actions, hardworking parents, loving fathers, devoted mothers, respectful children, happy families, gentle caregivers, honest employees, fair bosses, and such.

This applies in business, too, and has a direct impact on productivity and profitability. A team of psychologists visited sixty companies and transcribed every word in their business meetings. They then analyzed each sentence for positive or negative words and worked out the ratio of positive to negative statements. Their conclusion? "There is a sharp dividing line. Companies with better than a 3:1 ratio for positive to negative statements are flourishing. Below that ratio, companies are not doing well economically. But don't go overboard with positivity. Life is a ship with sails and rudder. Above 13:1, without a negative rudder, the positive sails flap aimlessly, and you lose your credibility."[1]

Purity, Not Filth

"Whatsoever things are pure." When was the last time you saw a film that celebrated Christian marriage or that portrayed a normal functioning family? Immorality, abuse, fighting, and murder rule the day. Filth floats to the surface while purity sinks without a trace.

Make the choice and take the steps to move the spotlight to happy and godly relationships, long and faithful marriages, and so on. Rejoice over the many godly young people who do not use porn,

---

1. Martin Seligman, *Flourish* (New York: Simon & Schuster, 2011), Kindle locations 1113–1120.

who do not dress immodestly, who keep their hearts with all diligence, and who keep themselves pure until marriage.

Beautiful, Not Ugly

"Whatsoever things are lovely" describes what is attractive and winsome, words and actions that compel admiration and affection. Perhaps the best modern word would be *beautiful*—hardly a word that comes to mind when we watch TV or surf the Internet, is it?

In a day when many of us live among steel and concrete boxes of varying sizes and shapes, it's often very difficult to locate beauty in our immediate surroundings. At best, our eyes feast on the mundane and the monotonous; at worst, on decay and brokenness. Our noses are blocked with dust and grime, our ears are assailed with traffic and jackhammers, and our taste buds are dulled with mass-produced junk food.

We need to get out of the city, see the stunning mountains, savor the fragrance of the forest, taste the thrill of fresh and healthy produce, and listen to the exquisite birdsong. And if that's too difficult, then we can get a BBC documentary like *Planet Earth* or *Deep Sea*. You can travel our beautiful world and plunge into our magnificent oceans from the comfort of your favorite armchair. Find ways to increase your intake of beauty through your various senses.

Praise, Not Complaint

When Paul calls us to think on "whatsoever things are of good report," he is saying, "Focus on what is constructive rather than destructive." We should feast on whatever makes people exclaim, "Well done!" rather than what makes us and others say, "That's terrible."

As you drive with your family, do you suggest topics that will show people in a good light or in a bad light? Do you tell stories that will make your hearers praise God and others or that will make people doubt God and condemn others? Do you shield your children from the destructively critical spirit of talk radio and substitute stimulating and inspiring conversation? Do you thank God for the national reduction in crime, the worldwide rise in literacy, and so on?

There is much good in everyday life that should be acknowledged and appreciated, regardless of whether it is done by a Christian or not. Whether it's a good product, a helpful service, a wise insight, or a superb article, we should praise and celebrate it. Don't look for what you can critique; look for what you can admire, and invite others to enjoy it with you. As an experiment, why not try to go twenty-four hours without speaking negatively about anything or anyone. Instead, fill these hours with hopeful and optimistic words. To do this every day would be imbalanced and unrealistic, but to do it for a few days might help to right your listing ship and set it on a more balanced course.

As Paul puts it in his summary of these six criteria, "If there be *any* virtue, and if there be *any* praise, think on these things" (v. 8).

Even secular sources are recognizing the harmful effects of most news media. In "News is bad for you—and giving it up will make you happier," *The Guardian's* Rolf Dobelli argues that news "leads to fear and aggression, and hinders your creativity and ability to think deeply." He says it misleads, is toxic to your body, increases cognitive errors, inhibits thinking, wastes time, makes us passive, and kills creativity.[2]

Some Christians might need to know more of the details about major disasters and tragedies, especially those whom God has especially called to interpret and explain these monstrous actions to the public and the church. But most of us don't need to glue ourselves to the TV and to Internet news. Instead, we should actively shield ourselves and our families from much of it.

But won't that mean ignoring problems in the real world? Quite the reverse, says Professor Shawn Achor: "Psychologists have found that people who watch less TV are actually more accurate judges of life's risks and rewards than those who subject themselves to the tales of crime, tragedy, and death that appear night after night on the ten o'clock news. That's because these people are less likely to see sensationalized or one-sided sources of information, and thus see reality more clearly."[3]

I have gotten to the point where I read only a couple of headlines and perhaps the first paragraph of most reports about mass killings, tsunamis, terrorism, and such. I operate on a "need to know" basis,

---

2. Rolf Dobelli, "News is bad for you—and giving it up will make you happier," *The Guardian*, April 12, 2013, http://www.guardian.co.uk/media/2013/apr/12/news -is-bad-rolf-dobelli?CMP=twt_gu (accessed July 15, 2013).

3. Shawn Achor, cited in Gretchen Rubin, *The Happiness Project* (New York: Harper, 2011), 53.

and I don't need to know everything. To me, that's putting Philippians 4:8 into practice.

And practice it we must. This was not just a theory for Paul; he could appeal to the Philippians' memory of him: "Those things, which ye have both learned, and received, and heard, and seen in me, do: and the God of peace shall be with you" (v. 9). He says that if we think like he thinks and do what he does, we will replace fear, anxiety, depression, and worry with divine peace.

Ministry Diet

But it's not just the diet that the world feeds us that we have to be concerned about; we need to guard our spiritual stomachs as well. These criteria must also be applied to the ministries under which we sit and the spiritual resources we read, listen to, and watch.

If we are in ministry roles ourselves—preacher, teacher, Sunday school teacher, or even a parent—we must also ask if the diet we are feeding Christ's sheep meets Paul's checklist. What should we be feeding on or feeding to others? Using Paul's criteria, I would suggest a rebalancing along the following lines.

More Salvation Than Sin

Unless people are taught the doctrine of sin and experience conviction of sin, the gospel makes no sense to them and has no power. Despite many wanting to downplay sin, minimize God's law, and soften God's anger, the gospel message must begin with "All have sinned, and come short of the glory of God" (Rom. 3:23).

However, we don't want to linger there any longer than we have to. Some preachers, teachers, and parents love to dwell in the smoke and fire of Mount Sinai more than the love and grace of Mount Calvary. They want us not only to see and smell the prodigal's pigsty, but to linger and wallow in its gruesome details. Sin is bad enough without sensationalistic overconcentration on some of the most evil atrocities.

Without losing the essential backdrop of our desperate human need, let's keep the spotlight on the multidimensional salvation that Christ has purchased. There are so many wonderful ways to describe it, picture it, and experience it. "God sent not his Son into the world to condemn the world; but that the world through him might be saved" (John 3:17).

More Truth Than Falsehood

Just as banks train tellers to spot counterfeit money by overexposing them to real money, and doctors are trained to detect heart and lung disease by listening to thousands of healthy chests, so Christians would be more edified and better prepared to spot falsehood by focusing the majority of their reading and teaching on *the truth* rather than trying to know and counteract the innumerable errors, heresies, false religions, and cults that fill our world.

Yes, we need to know what's wrong about other people's worldviews and theologies, but we need far more to know what's right in our own. Let's fill our minds with biblical truth, with the doctrines of grace, and with Scripture verses. Let's give more time to communicating the truth than to exposing error. Let's set forth the beautiful ethical directions of God's moral law much more than condemning infractions of it. Let's exalt biblical marriage far more than highlighting the latest perversion of it.

More Wooing Than Warning

Although every preacher must both woo and warn, the note of wooing should be more regular than the note of warning. There should be more of the carrot than the stick, more of the beauty of holiness than the ugliness of sin, more of the drawing of Christ than the danger of the devil, and more of the attraction of heaven than the fear of hell.

Let's present Christ to our congregations or to our children and colleagues in all His adorable glory. Show them how much Jesus is willing and able to save, and how much He desires and delights to save. He does not save because He has to do so but because He wants to do so and enjoys doing so.

It's often said that Jesus preached on hell more than *anyone* else. That's true. But He did not preach on hell more than *anything* else. Yes, He warned a lot, but He wooed and won even more.

More Victory Than Struggle

Trial, suffering, backsliding, defeat, and *temptation* are all biblical words, but so are *victory, growth, maturity, progress, usefulness, fruit, service, opportunity, advance,* and *encouragement.* Paul wanted to know "the fellowship of [Christ's] sufferings," but he also wanted to know "the power of his resurrection" (Phil. 3:10). He knew the continuing power of indwelling sin (Romans 7), but he also knew the breaking of sin's dominion and the power of life in the Spirit (Romans 8). Do our sermons, blog posts, prayers, and songs reflect this biblical emphasis?

Yes, we want to gently sympathize with strugglers, the discouraged, and the defeated. But we don't want to make a virtue of these experiences, as if they are preferable to growth, assurance, joy, and so on. We don't want to break the bruised reed or quench the smoking flax, but we don't want people to remain bruised and smoking either. We want to come alongside, splint their brokenness, fan their embers, and encourage them upward and forward.

Yes, we want to identify with and sympathize with the persecuted. But we must also inform ourselves and others of the number of people coming to faith in different countries and the impact of the gospel around the world.

More Celebration Than Lamentation
It's easy for Christians to be sucked down into the vortex of moaning and groaning about the direction of our culture and society. I've been to prayer meetings that are just a litany of complaints about various government policies. Yes, there is a time to mourn, but there is also a time to laugh (Eccl. 3:4). When we consider how many blessings we have compared to so many, we must sometimes sound like spoiled children, whining, whining, and whining for more.

Bradley Wright describes how he was recently in the current-affairs section of an airport bookshop: "All [the books] argued to a greater or lesser extent that a) the world is a terrible place and b) it's getting worse.... I didn't see a single optimistic book."[4] He calls for a Christian contrast to this worldly pessimism: "Two thousand years ago, a book whose core was *euangelion*—good news—began to be widely read. We of all people should be able to recognize and celebrate and express gratitude wherever we find it. For all good news is God's good news, and to ignore it, hide it, minimize it, or distort it is neither mentally healthy nor spiritually sound."[5]

Of course, there is much to lament, but, as Christians, the note of celebration should usually be heard above the note of lamentation.

---

4. Bradley Wright, *Upside: Surprising Good News About the State of Our World* (Bloomington, Minn.: Bethany, 2011), 15.

5. Wright, *Upside*, 12.

We have so much to be thankful for in the present and even more in the future. Remember that the apostles even managed to celebrate that they were counted worthy to suffer persecution for Christ's sake (Acts 5:41)! They took literally the Lord's command to "rejoice and be exceeding glad" (Matt. 5:12) even in the midst of great suffering.

Conclusion

"As he thinketh in his heart, so is he," wrote Solomon (Prov. 23:7). We are what we think. Let's start a Philippians 4:8 mind diet and see how much healthier and happier we will become.

CHAPTER 11

Living through Sickness and Death

Brian Croft

Mark 5:21–43

In 2012, I had the privilege of preaching my grandmother's funeral. Her death was a shock to us all, as less than two months prior, even though she was eighty-five years old, she was playing ball with my children, carrying my young daughter around to help her water her flowers, visiting with her friends, working around her house, and serving her church. She, like us, had no idea how little time she had left. An aggressive cancer in her back changed all that.

Her death caused us to remember many things about life, yet the most significant reminder to us was how helpless and powerless we are to resist the effects of the fall in regard to sickness, suffering, and, ultimately, death. Undoubtedly, some of you, too, are reminded of this reality as you read this, as you or others you love are suffering and battling sickness, physical challenges, or a death that is near.

How are we to live our lives and find hope, knowing sickness, suffering, and death await us all? We find a clear and helpful answer in Mark 5.

Mark writes this gospel account to point us to the fact that Jesus is the Son of God and the One who ushers in the kingdom of God with His arrival. Because of this purpose, Mark spends most of his gospel account pointing to the authority of Jesus as the Son of God.

A significant verse that is the interpretive key for several of these events is found at the end of Mark 4. This is where the disciples, just after Jesus calmed the storm, asked one another, "What manner of man is this, that even the wind and the sea obey him?" (v. 41). Mark gives three answers to this question. The first is that

Jesus is sovereign—in other words, He rules—over nature (4:35–41). The second is that Jesus is sovereign over the spiritual realm (5:1–20). The third, arguably the one that troubles us the most, is that Jesus is sovereign over sickness and death (5:21–43). As we examine this passage, may God in His mercy give you comfort through His Word in whatever place of difficulty you find yourself.

> And when Jesus was passed over again by ship unto the other side, much people gathered unto him: and he was nigh unto the sea. And, behold, there cometh one of the rulers of the synagogue, Jairus by name; and when he saw him, he fell at his feet, and besought him greatly, saying, My little daughter lieth at the point of death: I pray thee, come and lay thy hands on her, that she may be healed; and she shall live. And Jesus went with him; and much people followed him, and thronged him. And a certain woman, which had an issue of blood twelve years, and had suffered many things of many physicians, and had spent all that she had, and was nothing bettered, but rather grew worse, when she had heard of Jesus, came in the press behind, and touched his garment. For she said, If I may touch but his clothes, I shall be whole. And straightway the fountain of her blood was dried up; and she felt in her body that she was healed of that plague. And Jesus, immediately knowing in himself that virtue had gone out of him, turned him about in the press, and said, Who touched my clothes? And his disciples said unto him, Thou seest the multitude thronging thee, and sayest thou, Who touched me? And he looked round about to see her that had done this thing. But the woman fearing and trembling, knowing what was done in her, came and fell down before him, and told him all the truth. And he said unto her, Daughter, thy faith hath made thee whole; go in peace, and be whole of thy plague. While he yet spake, there came from the ruler of the synagogue's house certain which said, Thy daughter is dead: why troublest thou the Master any further? As soon as Jesus heard the word that was spoken, he saith unto the ruler of the synagogue, Be not afraid, only believe. And he suffered no man to follow him, save Peter, and James, and John the brother of James. And he cometh to the house of the ruler of the synagogue, and seeth the tumult, and them that wept and wailed greatly. And when he was come in, he saith unto them, Why make ye this ado, and weep? the damsel is not dead, but sleepeth. And they laughed him to scorn. But when he had put them

all out, he taketh the father and the mother of the damsel, and them that were with him, and entereth in where the damsel was lying. And he took the damsel by the hand, and said unto her, Talitha cumi; which is, being interpreted, Damsel, I say unto thee, arise. And straightway the damsel arose, and walked; for she was of the age of twelve years. And they were astonished with a great astonishment. And he charged them straitly that no man should know it; and commanded that something should be given her to eat.

In this passage, Jesus gives us two answers to the question of how we should face the inevitability of sickness:

Trusting in Jesus' Sovereignty over Sickness
The first of these is that we should trust that Jesus is sovereign over sickness. We need hope in sickness, not only because it can lead to death, but also because some of the most helpless times of our lives are those when we see the effects of the fall through sickness upon someone we love and there is nothing we can do about it: when that encouraging elderly lady with a sharp mind is suddenly diagnosed with Alzheimer's disease; when that active, athletic man is stricken with miserable bouts of arthritis; or when, of all things, cancer is found in the pastor's wife while she carries their fourth child. We need hope for our lives in sickness, and it is the same hope those in our passage found—Jesus, the sovereign Ruler over all things, including sickness.

As Mark recounts, Jesus crossed over on a boat to the other side of the sea and was greeted once again by a great multitude (v. 21). In that multitude, we find a man named Jairus, who came to Him (v. 22). Jairus was an official who presided over the elders of the local synagogue. We also find a woman who had suffered from a hemorrhage for many years (v. 25). These two examples show the certainty of Jesus' sovereignty over sickness. Through these examples, I pray we as Christians may learn how to trust in our Savior and King in whatever sickness or difficulty we face.

This passage urges us to respond to Jesus in three ways. First, we must come to Jesus and depend on Him.

Jairus was a very important man in the Jewish synagogue. A brief survey of the early chapters of Mark reveals that the Pharisees and other religious leaders were growing in their hatred for Jesus. Accordingly, Jairus stood to face much adversity by coming to Jesus.

However, when we face sickness and death, is it not amazing that we seem to get a better perspective about what really matters in life? Jairus was not too concerned about his reputation once he realized his daughter was sick to the point of death (v. 23). He wanted her to be healed, and knew this Jesus was the only One who possessed the power to do so, which is why we see him fall at Jesus' feet (v. 22) and request that He come and lay His hand upon her (v. 23).

The woman with a twelve-year hemorrhage (v. 25) also came to Jesus for help. Because of this hemorrhage, she had lost everything (v. 26), was ceremonially unclean, and had lost all hope. She heard about Him (v. 27), and though there was a great crowd and she was told nothing could be done, she still came to Jesus.

Second, we must have great faith in Jesus. I do not know about you, but daily I find that something happens that shows how weak my faith really is. We need to be challenged by the faith of these two people.

Notice that the woman had such great faith in Jesus' ability to heal her that she thought, "If I may touch but his clothes, I shall be whole" (v. 28). For twelve years, no one had been able to help her. In fact, she was worse. Yet she believed that just touching the garments of Jesus, who is sovereign over sickness, could make her well. That is great faith.

We see the same with Jairus. His daughter was "at the point of death" (v. 23). He could have searched for a doctor. He could have stayed with his daughter so he would be by her side when she died. Yet what did he do? He took the long shot that he could find Jesus, get to Him in the midst of the great crowd, and convince Jesus to come to where his daughter was, all because he believed Jesus was the only One who could save her.

This was no ordinary faith. That was great faith. Not only was this great faith, but we see that it is this kind of faith that Jesus requires. He told the woman after she had been healed, "Thy faith hath made thee whole" (v. 34). He told Jairus after his daughter died, "Be not afraid, only believe" (v. 36).

Third, we must desire for Jesus' power and authority to be known. This is what Mark is communicating in this story by describing how this woman was healed. When she touched Jesus' garment, the flow of blood dried up and she was healed (v. 29). However, Jesus recognized that power had gone from Him and wanted to know who had touched Him (v. 30). So the woman fell down before Him and told Him it was she (v. 33). Mark is showing her great faith. But of even greater significance, he is displaying the great power and authority of Jesus over all things, including this long-term sickness that disappeared at just the touch of His garment.

Jesus' great power was also certainly known to the child He brought back to life. Imagine the scene. Those who had received the news of the little girl's death were loudly weeping and wailing. Then Jesus walked in and told them, "The damsel is not dead, but sleepeth" (v. 39).

Imagine being in the position of this little girl's family. What would we think if some stranger came unannounced to the visitation of our deceased loved one and said, "She is not dead, just asleep"? We would think he was crazy or was making the worst-timed joke in the history of the world. We certainly would not believe he was right.

No wonder they laughed at Jesus (v. 40). Yet Jesus displayed His great power and authority over sickness and death by raising the child.

For us, the question is not whether we will face sickness and physical pain, but how we will face it. If Jesus is sovereign over sickness, then we as Christians should react to sickness completely differently than the world does. If Jesus is in complete control over sickness, disease, and our physical struggles, then we need to consider the purposes and plans that Jesus has for us when we face sickness. Many questions will go unanswered, but in this passage Mark has revealed several that we can be certain Jesus is answering to mold and shape us in His image in those moments.

In sickness, Jesus wants us to trust in Him. We do so by coming to Him and depending upon Him with a great faith, not depending on ourselves. In the same way in which we depend upon sleep, food, and water to sustain our lives, we must faithfully depend upon Christ in daily life so that when sickness comes, we are already trusting in His good and perfect plan in it.

At the age of eighty-two, with his health fading, John Newton said, "It is a great thing to die; and, when flesh and heart fail, to have

God for the strength of our heart, and our portion forever."[1] One of the gifts of God in sickness is that it enables us to see clearer how much we live our lives depending upon ourselves and our own strength instead of upon Christ, who is our rest, refuge, and help in trouble.

God uses sickness to display His great power to achieve His purposes for His glory. Did you notice that in this passage, there was instant healing for the woman, but the little girl died? The girl's father had requested healing, but as Jesus talked with the woman who had touched His garment, the girl died. Did the girl die because Jesus lost track of time? Certainly not. Jesus purposed to display His power in the woman healed from a hopeless physical condition, and He purposed to raise a little girl from the dead to display His greatest power.

This account brings back memories of when my oldest daughter, Abby, was in the hospital with pneumonia and not doing well. I had a crisis of faith because I realized how years of preaching the sovereignty of God collided with this situation. Did I really believe what I preached? If I did, God could see fit to glorify Himself through taking her life.

I realized without a doubt that I really did believe that Jesus was sovereign over sickness; I just did not want to lose her. But I also realized that we cannot have a great faith in Jesus' sovereignty over sickness if we are not willing to accept His purposes for His glory. It was not until I finally had a peace in my heart that I was submissive to whatever God saw fit to do to glorify His name that she began to improve and God chose to spare her.

However, He may not choose to spare her tomorrow. In God's all-wise providence, He chose not to spare my grandmother. But whatever the outcome in your circumstance of sickness, it does not change the fact that Jesus rules over all things, including sickness—your sickness, your spouse's sickness, your child's sickness, your fellow church member's sickness, or your pastor's wife's sickness.

Christian friends, God is a good and compassionate God, and He will use your sickness in whatever way He sees fit to display His power and glory. The question is, are you submissive to whatever that is? My prayer for you is that you will have a great faith and experience a fellowship with our Savior like never before because

---

1. John Newton, cited in Richard Cecil, *Memoirs of the Rev. John Newton*, in *The Works of the Rev. John Newton* (Edinburgh: Banner of Truth, 1985), 1:89.

you are coming to Him and by faith you are trusting in Him and His purposes, knowing they are for your good and His glory.

Rejoicing in Jesus' Sovereignty over Death

The second answer Jesus gives us to the question of how we must face the inevitability of sickness is that we must rejoice that Jesus is sovereign over death. The crescendo of the four miracles we see in Mark 4–5 is found in this profound truth. Jesus rules over nature, the spiritual realm, and sickness, but Mark has saved the best and the most powerful of all for last. Jesus is sovereign over death, and upon this truth the gospel stands and our hope in this life is found. Just as the certainty of death is before us all, may we see the certainty of Jesus' power over death and rejoice.

Our passage reveals two ways we find our hope. First, we must not doubt Jesus' power. Mark develops the scene in Jairus's house just after his daughter died (v. 35ff). Notice what the messengers said to Jairus: "While he yet spake, there came from the ruler of the synagogue's house certain which said, Thy daughter is dead: why troublest thou the Master any further?" (v. 35). In other words, it was over. They felt Jairus's daughter was past the point where anyone, including Jesus, could do anything. Especially in sickness and death, how easily can we get to this point? Not even Jesus could help.

In this, we begin to see God's purpose, as Jesus told Jairus in response to their words of pessimism, "Be not afraid, only believe" (v. 36). It was in the midst of everyone weeping and wailing (v. 38) that Jesus took the child by the hand and said, "Damsel, I say unto thee, arise" (v. 41). She did. Are you not thankful that Jesus' power over all things, including death, is not limited to what we can conceive?

Second, we must believe Jesus is like us—but not like us. One of the essentials of our faith is that Jesus was fully human, yet He lived a perfectly sinless life. Otherwise, He could not have borne our sins in our place as He did on the cross, and then in exchange give us His righteousness by faith. However, we see in this passage one way that Jesus, though being completely human, is not like us. He has a power that every human being would do anything to possess—the ability to raise the dead.

The people in the house laughed and mocked Jesus when He said she was only sleeping (v. 40). Then, when Jesus raised her from the dead, Mark tells us, "They were astonished with a great astonishment" (v. 42). This is because, as strong and powerful as men have been throughout the ages, no one raises the dead. That is a power that only God Himself possesses. In this astounding act of power and authority, Jesus answered the question of Mark 4:41 and declared Himself the Son of the most high God and sovereign even over the grave.

We are all just like those in this passage—powerless to overcome death in any way. However, Jesus not only has power over death, but He died on the cross for our sins in our place and rose from the dead so that we can conquer death and the grave through Him; or, to consider how Paul explains it, "If we have been planted together in the likeness of his death, we shall be also in the likeness of his resurrection" (Rom. 6:5). Why would we place our hope and trust in anything or anyone other than the sovereign Son of God, who provided a way for us not only to be reconciled to our Creator, but to live eternally with Him, as sons and daughters of the living God? All of this is because of Christ.

Conclusion

Dear friend, if you are not a follower of Christ, why would you place your hope and trust in anything other than Christ? Do you actually think you will find hope in yourself when your mind or physical body is attacked and becomes frail? Will you trust in your presumed good works when you stand before our holy God and Creator to give an account for your many sins? Dear friend, God's Word is clear—you will not stand. I plead with you to fall upon the mercy of God and flee to Christ and away from the wrath to come. Experience the true hope we have in the One who rules over our sicknesses and conquered death on our behalf.

My grandmother was a faithful follower of Jesus and was a powerful testimony of this hope we have in our sovereign Savior, who conquered death on our behalf. I sat with her in the hospital the day after she received the news about the cancer. She acknowledged how hard this would be, but then declared her trust in Christ to see her through it. I saw that trust in Christ as the pain in her back became excruciating; she cried out to Jesus for comfort.

I also saw that trust in Jesus when I sat in the hospital with her the final day she was alert enough to have a conversation. She asked me to read God's Word to her. She believed Jesus was sovereign over her sickness, suffering, and death, and that faith empowered her to hold fast to Christ to the end (Heb. 3:14). Now she has the privilege to have fully experienced the words of Paul, "To live is Christ, and to die is gain" (Phil. 1:21).

Christian friends, this is the same place we find our hope and joy in the uncertainty of sickness and death. Whether you or someone you love is facing a great, physically debilitating struggle, cancer, or an incurable disease, hold fast to our sovereign Savior, knowing He is our hope, our joy, and the One who rules over the circumstances of our sickness and even our death for the good of His people, for the display of the gospel, and the glory of His great name.

CHAPTER 12

Living Hopefully in Hard Times: The Beauty and Glory of the Book of Judges

John W. Tweeddale

Judges is a hard but hopeful book. It is a hard book because it chronicles the sad story of spiritual decline within the household of faith. It pummels you with the unpleasant truth that the greatest threat to the people of God isn't an external one (in this case, the lure of Canaan) but an internal one (forgetful, disobedient, self-indulgent hearts). But, thankfully, Judges does more than that. The importance of this book goes far beyond its shock value in exposing the harsh reality about our own depravity. Judges is also a hopeful book. It doesn't simply recount a record of wrong. It broadcasts the tenacity of God's grace over the trauma of our sin.

The ancient tale of Israel's judges is as pertinent for the church today as when it was first written more than three millennia ago.[1] While it might not be the first place you would look for a description of the beauty and glory of Christian living, let me give you five reasons why studying Judges is essential for your spiritual growth.

First, the book of Judges is the Word of God. As the apostle Paul reminds us, the entire Old Testament was written "for our learning,

---

1. The author and date of Judges are unknown. However, given the repetitive "no king" references throughout the book (Judg. 17:6; 18:1; 19:1; 21:25), a strong case can be made that it was written before King David's reign. See Dale Ralph Davis, *Judges: Such a Great Salvation*, Focus on the Bible (Ross-shire, Scotland: Christian Focus, 2000), 200, n5; see also Gleason L. Archer, Jr., *A Survey of Old Testament Introduction*, rev. ed. (Chicago: Moody, 1985), 280–82; R. K. Harrison, *Introduction to the Old Testament* (Grand Rapids: Eerdmans, 1971), 682–90; George M. Schwab, *Right in Their Own Eyes: The Gospel According to Judges*, The Gospel According to the Old Testament (Phillipsburg, N.J.: P&R, 2011), 3–37.

that we through patience and comfort of the scriptures might have hope" (Rom. 15:4). God in His wisdom gave us Judges for our encouragement and endurance in the faith (Heb. 11:32). As Paul makes clear, "All scripture is given by inspiration of God, and is profitable for doctrine, for reproof, for correction, for instruction in righteousness: that the man of God may be perfect, thoroughly furnished unto all good works" (2 Tim. 3:16–17). Paul's teaching on the inspiration and sufficiency of Scripture does not apply only to those parts that make us feel spiritually warm and cozy; it refers to all of Sacred Writ. Judges is the inerrant, infallible, breathed-out Word of God, and is therefore profitable for us.

Second, the book of Judges paints an unsettling portrait of what the Puritans called the sinfulness of sin.[2] It is not like a typical painting you might find in an art gallery, an enigmatic piece of artwork for which you must supply your own subjective meaning. You don't interpret this portrait; it interprets you. Like a mirror that accentuates imperfections on your skin, Judges exposes blemishes on your soul. In doing so, it reveals your need of God's appointed deliverer, the Lord Jesus Christ. Perhaps this is one reason why Judges does not often make the cut of top ten books of the Bible; it has an uncanny way of confronting you with the ugliness of unbelief.

"There is much in Judges to sadden the heart of the reader," says Arthur Cundall. "Perhaps no book in the Bible witnesses so clearly to our human frailty."[3] The witness to human weakness is one of the profound lessons of the book of Judges. While texts such as Romans 1 and Ephesians 2 explain the doctrine of total depravity with razor-sharp precision, Judges expounds the same teaching with the compelling power of a true story. Like it or not, this is the history of God's people.

---

2. The phrase "sinfulness of sin" is well attested in Puritan literature and was used to underscore the vileness of our sinful nature. See the standard treatments by Jeremiah Burroughs, *Evil of Evils: The Exceeding Sinfulness of Sin* (Morgan, Pa.: Soli Deo Gloria, 1992); Edward Reynolds, *The Sinfulness of Sin*, in *The Works of Edward Reynolds*, 6 vols. (London: B. Holdsworth, 1826), 1:102–353; Ralph Venning, *The Sinfulness of Sin* (Edinburgh: Banner of Truth, 1993).

3. Arthur E. Cundall, "Judges," in Arthur E. Cundall and Leon Morris, *Judges and Ruth: An Introduction and Commentary*, Tyndale Old Testament Commentaries (Downers Grove, Ill.: InterVarsity Press, 2008), 11.

One of the reasons why biblical narratives are so important for the church is that they help us to place the flesh and blood of faith on the bones of biblical truth.[4] Judges purposefully contrasts the lines of sin and grace in bold relief. By learning to see the sinfulness of sin with greater clarity in the failings of Israel in Canaan, we are in a position to apprehend more fully the magnitude of God's grace and our need of it. That's why J. C. Ryle began his book *Holiness* with these well-known words:

> He that wishes to attain right views about Christian holiness must begin by examining the vast and solemn subject of sin. He must dig down very low if he would build high. A mistake here is most mischievous. Wrong views about holiness are generally traceable to wrong views about human corruption.... I am convinced that the first step towards attaining a higher standard of holiness is to realize more fully the amazing sinfulness of sin.[5]

Ryle is right. If we wish to excel in the beauty and glory of Christian living, the first step we must take is to "dig down very low" to examine the cavern of our own corruption. But we must tread carefully. The reason we dig down is not to wallow in the grime of sin but to wonder at the brilliance of God's grace.[6] What better place to start digging than Judges?

Third, the book of Judges gives us a stunning account of God's relentless pursuit of His people. The writer wants us to see that grace is more shocking than sin. What is not so surprising in this book is the predictable ways Israel slid into spiritual debauchery when enticed by the empty titillations of Canaanite idols. It's the same tired story of rebellion and self-centeredness that has plagued humanity since the fall of Adam and Eve. But what is unexpected is how God responded to His people's pleas of desperation with deliverance and

---

4. On the value of Old Testament narratives, see David Murray, *Jesus on Every Page: 10 Simple Ways to Seek and Find Christ in the Old Testament* (Nashville: Thomas Nelson, 2013), 99–114; for fuller discussions, see Dale Ralph Davis, *The Word Became Fresh: How to Preach from Old Testament Narrative Texts* (Ross-shire, Scotland: Mentor, 2006); Richard L. Pratt, *He Gave Us Stories: The Bible Student's Guide to Interpreting Old Testament Narratives* (Phillipsburg, N.J.: P&R, 1993).

5. J. C. Ryle, *Holiness* (Darlington, England: Evangelical Press, 1999), 1, 14.

6. Compare the statement of Edward Reynolds, "The exceeding sinfulness of sin might serve both the sooner to compel men to come to Christ, and the grace of Christ might thereby appear to be more exceeding gracious." Reynolds, *Works*, 1:120.

forgiveness. As Richard Gamble states, "The ultimately beautiful part of the story of Judges, both then and now, is the great compassion of God, who was and is long-suffering and compassionate."[7] Judges is such a thrilling book because it catapults you out of the mire of sin and into the arms of God.

Fourth, the book of Judges serves as a redemptive-historical bridge that links the patriarchs and the kings. Within the biblical canon, the books of Joshua and Judges record for us life in Israel between Moses and David (much like the book of Acts chronicles events in the church between Jesus and Paul). While Joshua highlights Israel's faithfulness in conquering Canaan, Judges underscores Israel's faithlessness in becoming like Canaan. It covers an approximately 350-year period of spiritual decline. The church has much to learn from this period in Israel's history. Judges teaches us lessons about the disintegration of faith as Israel abandoned God's promises and absorbed Canaanite practices, the importance of God-given leadership for spiritual growth, the centrality of repentance for overcoming sin and temptation, and the doggedness of God in not forsaking His covenant people.

Finally, the book of Judges provides an argument for kingship in Israel. By depicting a land of anarchy where there is no king, no rule, and no order, and where everyone does what is right in his own eyes, this book makes you long for Israel's King. It builds the case for a monarch who does what is right in God's eyes. The importance of Judges lies not only in the fact that it establishes why Israel needed David to rescue them but also why we need David's greater Son to deliver us.

With these reasons in mind, let's turn our attention to the teaching of the text. The narrative breaks into three sections: a summary of the book is sketched in 1:1–3:6; the ministries of the twelve judges are recorded in 3:7–16:31; and the downward spiral of Israel is depicted in chapters 17–21.[8] We will focus on the opening section, since it provides a lens through which to read the unfolding plotline.

---

7. Richard C. Gamble, *The Whole Counsel of God: Volume 1: God's Mighty Acts in the Old Testament* (Phillipsburg, N.J.: P&R, 2009), 481.

8. Many commentators follow this basic outline. For example, see Daniel Block, *Judges, Ruth*, The New American Commentary (Nashville: B&H, 1999), 72–73; Davis, *Judges*, 12; Barry G. Webb, *The Book of Judges*, The New International Commentary on the Old Testament (Grand Rapids: Eerdmans, 2012), 32–35.

In particular, Judges 2:6–3:6 gives us a theological description of Israel's decline. From these verses, we glean at least four overall lessons from the book of Judges.

Forgetting God

Judges opens on a dark note. Joshua had died. Unlike when Moses died and passed the mantel of leadership to Joshua, there was no apparent successor in Israel (compare Josh. 1:1–9 and Judg. 1:1; 2:6–10). There was a crisis in the land. God's people were leaderless and defenseless. In a word, they seemed vulnerable.

The prospect of a future in Canaan with no commander in chief created anxiety within the tribes of Israel. You can imagine the questions they asked in Joshua's absence: "Who will shepherd us in the Promised Land? Who will oversee our future? Who will teach us God's law? Who will fight against our enemies?"

This was a moment of testing for Israel (Judg. 3:1, 4). How they responded to this leaderless scenario would set them on a path of faithfulness or unfaithfulness in the Promised Land. So what did the tribes do? Starting with Judah, they prayed, took up arms, and warred against the Canaanites in the knowledge that the Lord had given the enemy into their hands (Judg. 1:2). So far, so good.

The turning point, however, comes in Judges 1:19: "And the LORD was with Judah; and he drave out the inhabitants of the mountain; but could not drive out the inhabitants of the valley, because they had chariots of iron."

It seems so small, so subtle, and so insignificant, doesn't it?

God was with the people of Judah. But they couldn't get the job done. Astounding! These two incongruous statements provide a window into the heart of Israel (and us). God's people benefited from His covenant presence, yet they were immobilized by Canaan's superior military technology. They were dumbfounded into disobedience.

Paralyzed by the fear of being crushed by Canaanite chariots, Judah disregarded the fact that they had an even greater force multiplier: God was with them. Four times the Lord reminded His people of His presence (Judg. 1:2, 4, 19, 22). Yet despite these assurances, the Israelites could not drive out their enemies. The reason? The enemy had chariots of iron (v. 19). Judah and the other tribes did not obey because they believed God was outclassed by the Canaanites. Such unbelief is excruciatingly foolish.

Why did Israel equivocate? Could they not remember what took place in Jericho under the leadership of Joshua (Joshua 6)? The parallels are striking. At Jericho, they also had no great army, no advanced technology, no military weaponry, and no tactical advantage. Yet the walls came tumbling down. Why? Because the Lord was with Joshua and fought the battle of Jericho (contrast Josh. 6:27 and Judg. 1:19). How short was the memory of the people of God!

Israel's forgetfulness is the key to understanding her spiritual decline (cf. Deut. 4:23; 8:19; 1 Sam. 12:9). The tragedy of the book of Judges is that in the face of adversity, Israel forgot God's promises. As a result, a pattern of defiance emerged. The Lord repeatedly assured the people of His presence, yet they habitually discounted His promise. Joshua had even warned Israel against the danger of neglecting God's pledge to defeat their enemies (see Josh. 23:5–13). But they did not listen.

Failure to heed Joshua's counsel proved deleterious for Israel. Trent Butler has argued: "The book of Judges clearly and consciously reverses all that Joshua accomplished. In a real sense, the death of Joshua represents the death of Israel."[9] On the heels of Joshua's funeral, we read these harrowing words in Judges 2:10–12 and 3:7:

> And also all that generation were gathered unto their fathers: and there arose another generation after them, which knew not the LORD, nor yet the works which he had done for Israel. And the children of Israel did evil in the sight of the LORD, and served Baalim: And they forsook the LORD God of their fathers, which brought them out of the land of Egypt, and followed other gods, of the gods of the people that were round about them, and bowed themselves unto them, and provoked the LORD to anger.... And the children of Israel did evil in the sight of the LORD, and forgat the LORD their God, and served Baalim and the groves.

Why did the children of Israel do evil in the sight of the Lord? Why did they forsake God? Why did they serve Baalim? The answer,

---

9. Trent Butler, *Judges*, Word Biblical Commentary (Nashville: Thomas Nelson, 2009), lvii.

we are told, is that they forgot the Lord their God. God-forgetfulness is the prelude to God-forsakenness.

Israel's God-forgetfulness did not mean that the knowledge of God was expunged from the people's memory bank. Many could probably still recite the Sinai Shorter Catechism (Deut. 6:4–5). Evidence of this can be seen throughout the book of Judges, as Israel clearly had enough sense to cry out to God in moments of need. Israel's sin was not theological amnesia but apathy. As Daniel Block has shown, the Hebrew word translated as "forgot" in Joshua 3:7 means "to disregard, not to take into account."[10] Who needed the old-fashioned God of the exodus when Canaan had the seductive gods of fertility!

God-forgetfulness means disregarding God by failing to take into account His Word. The process is a subtle one. Once you may have been enthralled by grace and amazed by the gospel, but over time, you settle for lesser pleasures. Bedazzled by the Baalim, you become ambivalent toward the one true God. His Word no longer delights you. Instead, you languidly yawn in His face in deference to almost anything else, whether it is lust, ambition, greed, or whatever. You disengage from the beauty and glory of Christian living because you discount the beauty and glory of God. As Dietrich Bonhoeffer explains, "At this moment God loses all reality.... Satan does not fill us with hatred of God, but with forgetfulness of God."[11]

The temptation of God-forgetfulness was not unique to Israel. We are equally prone to disregard the promise of Christ as Immanuel, who has pledged to be with us as we carry out God's mission, just as the Lord had promised to be with Israel (see Matt. 1:23; 28:20). The enemy may no longer have chariots of iron, but we still act as though the odds are stacked against us in fulfilling the Great Commission. God forbid that we smugly shrug our shoulders in unbelief as though Christ's presence means nothing. Certainly this is one reason why Jesus beckoned us to remember Him at the Lord's Table (see 1 Cor. 11:24–25). If we do not, we will forget him. For this reason, the well-known words of John Newton, the one-time slave trader and author of "Amazing Grace," serve as an important corrective when

---

10. Block, *Judges, Ruth*, 151.
11. Dietrich Bonhoeffer, *Creation and Fall; Temptation: Two Biblical Studies* (New York: Touchstone, 1997), 132.

we are tempted to forget and forsake Immanuel. Toward the end of his life (in his eighties), he conveyed to a friend, "My memory is nearly gone, but I remember two things: that I am a great sinner and that Christ is a great Savior."[12] Remembering the cross of Christ is the only antidote to spiritual apathy.

The first, and in many ways most important, lesson of the book of Judges is that God's people sin by forgetting His Word.

Remembering Repentance

While we may forget God's promises, mercifully, He does not. The second lesson that Judges teaches us is that God calls His people to repentance. This theme is seen in Judges 3:7–11.

In these verses, we meet the first of twelve judges: a little-known figure named Othniel, who also happened to be the nephew of Caleb, the great Israelite spy. Not only does he represent a link to Israel's brighter past, he also serves as a "cookie-cutter" judge in that the rest of the book follows the basic pattern of his ministry. In the Othniel sequence, we witness a five-part series of events that epitomizes Israel's experience in Canaan: rebellion, reckoning, return, restoration, and rest.

Rebellion. Judges 3:7 states, "And the children of Israel did evil in the sight of the LORD, and forgat the LORD their God, and served Baalim and the groves." As we have seen, Israel rebelled against God by forgetting or neglecting His Word (Judg. 2:1–3, 16–17). They believed that they could live without reference to God's standard and do what was right in their own eyes (Judg. 17:6; 21:25). However, failure to heed God's Word is no peccadillo. The text is unambiguous: disobedience is evil in the sight of the Lord.[13] Rebellion begins when we belittle God's Word.

Reckoning. As a result of Israel's rebellion, we see a reckoning whereby God justly punished their sin. Verse 8 states, "Therefore

---

12. Quoted in Jonathan Aitken, *John Newton: From Disgrace to Amazing Grace* (Wheaton, Ill.: Crossway, 2007), 347.

13. The statement that Israel did what was "evil in sight of the LORD" runs as a refrain throughout Judges. Israel's evil is not simply defined in terms of their serving foreign gods but also, more fundamentally, of their disregarding God's Word. See in context Judges 2:11; 3:12; 4:1; 6:1; 10:6; 13:1. Compare these verses to similar texts in Num. 32:13; Deut. 4:25; 31:29; 1 Sam. 15:19. Forsaking Yahweh and serving Baal is the effect, not the cause, of Israel's forgetting God's Word.

the anger of the LORD was hot against Israel, and he sold them into the hand of Chushan-rish-a-thaim king of Mesopotamia: and the children of Israel served Chushan-rish-a-thaim eight years." While references to God's anger may cause us to bristle, we must not confuse His anger with an irrational fly-off-the-handle fit of rage. His wrath represents the intense passion He has for His glory and the good of His people. The Lord's actions are fully in keeping with His righteous character. He repeatedly told Israel that there would be consequences for their rebellion (see Deut. 7; Josh. 23:11–13; Judg. 2:1–2, 20–23). If they rejected Him, He would reject them. Lest we think this notion of divine punishment is confined to the Old Testament, we find this same line of reasoning in Jesus. He likewise states, "Whosoever shall deny me before men, him will I also deny before my Father which is in heaven" (Matt. 10:33; cf. Mark 8:38; 2 Thess. 1:5–10).

Return. In response to God's punishment, Israel returned to Him in repentance. Verse 9 states, "And...the children of Israel cried unto the LORD." Israel was bankrupt. The promise of paganism had proved hollow. The Baalim could not redeem them from the wicked hands of Chushan-rish-a-thaim.[14] The only thing Israel could do was cry out to the one they had abandoned. Eight years under a despot had showed them how much they needed a deliverer. God's chastening became the occasion for His people's repentance. Israel cried and God redeemed. He met their plea with open arms. There is great comfort in this text for the Lord's delinquent people. We must not take lightly the Father's discipline, even if it stings for eight hard years (Heb. 12:5–6). It may be the very thing we need to loosen our grasp on sin so that we might cry out to Him in repentance.

Rescue. Following repentance came restoration. Verses 9–10 state: "And when the children of Israel cried unto the LORD, the LORD raised up a deliverer to the children of Israel, who delivered them, even Othniel the son of Kenaz, Caleb's younger brother. And the Spirit of the LORD came upon him, and he judged Israel, and went out to war: and the LORD delivered Chushan-rish-a-thaim king of Mesopotamia into

---

14. The name Chushan-rish-a-thaim literally means "Chushan-of-double-wickedness" and was probably not the real name of the king of Mesopotamia. It was likely given by the author, or someone else in Israel, in jest. Who says the redeemed can't poke fun at the enemy? See Block, *Judges, Ruth*, 153; Webb, *The Book of Judges*, 159.

his hand; and his hand prevailed against Chushan-rish-a-thaim."
We have here the history of redemption in miniature. The pattern
is one we see throughout the Bible. God's people were in distress. In
response, the Lord graciously sent His Spirit-anointed servant to rescue His people from the enemy. This time, the deliverer was Othniel.
Ultimately, it will be Christ (Isa. 42:1; Matt. 12:15–21).

Rest. The Othniel episode ended fairly well. Verse 11 states: "And
the land had rest forty years. And Othniel the son of Kenaz died." To
Israel's great relief, God's servant Othniel secured rest from the enemy.
The nation was no longer at war. The land was at peace. The people
were finally enjoying life in the Promised Land as it was intended to
be (see Josh. 21:43–45). Sadly, however, the party was only short-lived.
After forty short years, rest came to an end (contrast Heb. 4:8–9).

The cycle of rebellion, reckoning, return, rescue, and rest repeats
several times throughout Judges. But as we go through the book, the
sequence deteriorates. Israel's infatuation with Canaan increased.
There came a point when they no longer cried out. By the end of the
book, there was no rest, no rescue, and no repentance. As a result, we
read these haunting words in Judges 10:13: "Yet ye have forsaken me,
and served other gods: wherefore I will deliver you no more."

One of the most dangerous things someone can do is presume
upon grace in order to perpetuate sin (see Ps. 19:13; Rom. 6:1). Statements such as "God will forgive me" may lead you into greater peril
if used to justify continued sinful behavior. You must not put off
repentance: "Today if ye will hear his voice, harden not your hearts"
(Heb. 4:7). The good news of Judges is that God does redeem and forgive those who trust in His Spirit-anointed deliverer (Acts 3:19). But
you must deal with your sin today, not tomorrow. Now is the time to
cry out to the Lord.

Judging Judges

The third point that Judges makes is that God delivers His people
through His appointed servants. The book surveys the ministries
of twelve Judges: Othniel, Ehud, Shamgar, Deborah/Barak, Gideon,
Tola, Jair, Jepthah, Ibzan, Elon, Abdon, and Samson. Each one was
associated with a different tribe.

When we hear the word *judge*, we typically think of someone
who sits behind a bench adjudicating cases in a court of law. While

the biblical judges were certainly concerned with upholding justice, we need a slightly different model to understand their role within Israel. The image you should have is more akin to John Knox with a sword in hand guarding George Wishart than a distinguished judge in a stoic gown. The biblical judges were guardians of God's people. Their motto, with apologies to Mr. Knox, was "Give me Israel, or I die." Their responsibility was twofold: uphold God's law and deliver His people from their enemies. When you read their stories, at least two things stand out.

First, God uses seemingly insignificant people to care for His people. We know very little about most of the judges. Take Tola and Jair in chapter 10. Hardly any information is given about them. Yet in God's kindness, He used them to bring a total of forty-five years of stability in Israel. While their lives are unfamiliar to us, I suspect if you had sat under their ministries, you would have seen them as stalwarts. God's people seem to thrive under faithful yet inconsequential servants (Col. 1:7; 4:12). The names John Black and Charlie Holiday probably don't mean anything to you. But for the congregation I serve, they were the first and ninth pastors; together they represent a total of eighty-eight years of marriages, baptisms, funerals, Bible studies, Sunday school lessons, worship services, and so on. History will not remember most of God's "insignificant" servants, yet their faithfulness represents stability for His people.

Second, God uses wildly flawed people to care for His people. The judges whom we know something about were not very impressive. Ehud was an assassin. Barak was a weakling. Gideon was an idolater. Jephthah was a son of a prostitute. And Samson was a womanizing Nazarite. Nevertheless, they were not only used to liberate Israel but have been celebrated for their faith (see 1 Sam. 12:10–11; Heb. 11:32–34). In His wisdom, God took a people whose chief sin was forgetting Him and redeemed them in unforgettable ways. You can almost hear the stories around Israel's campfires: "Remember when lefty Ehud stuck it to ol' fat Eglon (Judg. 3:12–30) or when the Lord used wimpy Barak to rout Sisera (Judg. 4–5)?" "How about when a love-struck, eye-gouged Samson brought down over three thousand Philistines" (Judg. 13–16)? How could we ever forget!" It should not surprise us then that this same God would ultimately send His sinless Son to redeem His people in an even more memorable way. He was born not in a palace but in a manger. He became the child not of a mighty ruler but of a virgin girl. He conquered sin not with a sword but with a cross. He defeated death not with modern medicine but with an empty tomb. How could we ever forget!

Slouching toward Canaan

The final lesson of Judges is that sin, when left unchecked, has devastating consequences for God's people. Under the judges, Israel spiraled out of control. As you read this tragic story, you discover that Israel indulged in nearly every imaginable evil, from blatant syncretism and rampant paganism to the butchering of a Levite concubine and full-blown civil war. By the end, Israel looks more like Canaan than the people of God. To tweak a phrase from Robert Bork, Israel was slouching toward Canaan.[15]

The warning of Judges is that unrestrained sin always aims at the uppermost manifestation of itself. In the words of the Puritan John Owen:

> Sin aims always at the utmost; every time it rises up to tempt or entice, might it have its own course, it would go out to the utmost sin in that kind. Every unclean thought or glance would be adultery if it could; every covetous desire would be oppression, every thought of unbelief would be atheism, might it grow to its head.[16]

No matter what sin you are struggling with today, do not let that sin linger in your heart. Take your sin to Christ before it takes you over. No matter how great your sin, your Savior is greater. Like the Thessalonians, we must turn "to God from idols to serve the living and true God; and to wait for his Son from heaven, whom he raised from the dead, even Jesus, which delivered us from the wrath to come" (1 Thess. 1:9–10).

Running toward Calvary

Judges vividly depicts the trauma of sin and the tenacity of God's grace. Understanding both of these truths is essential for us to grasp

---

15. Robert Bork, *Slouching towards Gomorrah* (New York: HarperCollins, 1997). The process of Israel's "Canaanization" is well documented in Block, *Judges, Ruth*, 58.

16. John Owen, "Mortification of Sin," in *The Works of John Owen*, 24 vols., ed. William H. Goold (Edinburgh: Banner of Truth, 1965), 6:12.

the beauty and glory of Christian living. As D. Martyn Lloyd-Jones has stated:

> The church has always triumphed and had her greatest success when she has preached the two-fold message of the depravity of human nature and the absolute necessity of the direct intervention of God for its final salvation.[17]

That, in a nutshell, describes the central message of the book of Judges. So, take this book in hand, learn from it, and then pray for strength and grace to do more than slouch toward Canaan. Pray that you may exemplify the beauty and glory of Christian living, by God's amazing grace, all the way until you reach that land where there will be no more slouching, no more wrestling with inward sin, no more imperfection and failure—indeed, where Christ will be all in all, and through Him the triune God Himself will be the beauty and glory of living forevermore. Then, dear believer, you will live in everlasting union with your worthy triune God in that heavenly land of Canaan where all good and beauty will be walled in and all evil and failure will be walled out.

---

17. D. Martyn Lloyd-Jones, *Evangelistic Sermons* (Edinburgh: Banner of Truth, 1983), 1.

Contributors

DR. MICHAEL BARRETT is academic dean and professor of Old Testament at Puritan Reformed Theological Seminary. He is a minister in the Free Presbyterian Church of North America. Formerly, Dr. Barrett served as president of Geneva Reformed Seminary. He has published numerous articles in both professional and popular journals. His other published works include *Beginning at Moses: A Guide to Finding Christ in the Old Testament*; *Complete in Him: A Guide to Understanding and Enjoying the Gospel*; *God's Unfailing Purpose: The Message of Daniel*; *The Beauty of Holiness: A Guide to Biblical Worship*; *Love Divine and Unfailing: The Gospel According to Hosea*; and *The Hebrew Handbook*. Dr. Barrett and his wife, Sandra, have two sons and five grandchildren.

DR. JOEL R. BEEKE is president and professor of systematic theology and homiletics at Puritan Reformed Theological Seminary; a pastor of the Heritage Netherlands Reformed Congregation in Grand Rapids, Michigan; editor of *Banner of Sovereign Grace Truth*; editorial director of Reformation Heritage Books; president of Inheritance Publishers; and vice-president of the Dutch Reformed Translation Society. He has written, co-authored, or edited seventy books (most recently, *A Puritan Theology: Doctrine for Life*; *Parenting by God's Promises: How to Raise Children in the Covenant of Grace*; *Living for the Glory of God: An Introduction to Calvinism*), and has contributed two thousand articles to Reformed books, journals, periodicals, and encyclopedias. He blogs at *Doctrine for Life*. Dr. Beeke and his wife, Mary, have three children.

DR. GERALD M. BILKES is professor of New Testament and biblical theology at Puritan Reformed Theological Seminary. He is an ordained minister in the Free Reformed Churches of North America. He has written *Glory Veiled and Unveiled: A Heart-Searching Look at Christ's Parables* and *Memoirs of the Way Home: Ezra and Nehemiah as a Call to Conversion*. He and his wife, Michelle, have five children.

BRIAN CROFT is senior pastor of Auburndale Baptist Church (ABC) in Louisville, Kentucky, and is the founder and ministry development director of Practical Shepherding, Inc. He is the author of *Visit the Sick: Ministering*

God's Grace in Times of Illness; *Test, Train, Affirm and Send into Ministry: Recovering the Local Church's Responsibility in the External Call*; *Help! He's Struggling with Pornography*; *Conduct Gospel-Centered Funerals: Applying the Gospel at the Unique Challenges of Death*; *A Faith That Endures: Meditations on Hebrews 11*; and *The Pastor's Family*, co-written with his wife, Cara. Pastor Croft and his wife have four children.

DR. IAN HAMILTON serves as minister of Cambridge Presbyterian Church, England, and formerly in Loudoun Church of Scotland, Ayrshire. He is a trustee of Banner of Truth and a board member of Greenville Presbyterian Theological Seminary and London Theological Seminary. He is an adjunct professor at GPTS and author of *The Erosion of Calvinist Orthodoxy: Drifting from the Truth in Confessional Scottish Churches*; *The Letters of John*; *John Calvin's Doctrine of Holy Scripture*; and *The Faith-Shaped Life*. Dr. Hamilton and his wife, Joan, have four children.

DR. DAVID P. MURRAY is professor of Old Testament and practical theology at Puritan Reformed Theological Seminary and is a pastor of the Free Reformed Church in Grand Rapids. He is the author of *Christians Get Depressed Too* and *How Sermons Work*, and the co-producer of *God's Technology: Training Our Children to Use Technology to God's Glory*. He also blogs at *Head Heart Hand*. Dr. Murray and his wife, Shona, have five children.

BRIAN G. NAJAPFOUR is the pastor of Dutton United Reformed Church in Caledonia, Michigan, and a doctoral student. He is co-editor of *Taking Hold of God: Reformed and Puritan Perspectives on Prayer* and author of *The Very Heart of Prayer: Reclaiming John Bunyan's Spirituality*, and *Jonathan Edwards: His Doctrine of and Devotion to Prayer*. He and his wife, Sarah, have one daughter.

JOHN W. TWEEDDALE is the senior pastor of First Reformed Presbyterian Church (PCA) in Pittsburgh and also serves as adjunct professor of church history at Reformed Presbyterian Theological Seminary. He has contributed to *The Ashgate Research Companion to John Owen's Theology* as well as written articles for *Tabletalk*, *The Banner of Truth Magazine*, and *reformation21*. Along with Dr. Derek Thomas, he has coauthored *The Essential Commentaries for a Preacher's Library*, revised edition, and co-edited *John Calvin: For a New Reformation*. He and his wife have three children.

DR. WILLIAM VANDOODEWAARD serves as associate professor of church history at Puritan Reformed Theological Seminary. He is the author of *The Marrow Controversy and Seceder Tradition*, a contributing editor for the recent reprint of Edward Fisher's *The Marrow of Modern Divinity*, and has written for several historical and theological journals. Dr. VanDoodewaard is an ordained minister in the Associate Reformed Presbyterian Churches. He and his wife, Rebecca, blog at *The Christian Pundit*, and they have three children.